The Anatomy of a Slogan

by

David Porter

With a Foreword by David Alton MP

OM Publishing
Carlisle, U.K.

British Library Cataloguing in Publication Data

Porter, David
Back to Basics
I. Title
261.7

1–85078–155–9

OM Publishing is an imprint of Send the Light Ltd.,
PO Box 300, Carlisle, Cumbria, CA3 0QS, U.K.

Cover design: Mainstream

Phototypeset by Intype, London
and Printed in the UK for
OM Publishing, PO Box 300, Carlisle, Cumbria, CA3 0QS
by Cox and Wyman Ltd, Reading.

CONTENTS

To Eleanor and Lauren, Péter and Máté:
For the future

FOREWORD

The Prime Minister, John Major, intended to change the moral climate by instigating his 'Back to Basics' campaign. But it didn't take long to sour and, amidst the debris and even tragedy, he soon began to rue the day his word-smiths and tacticians dreamt up this diversion into shark-infested waters. A short way into the campaign there was an announcement from him that 'Back to Basics' wasn't about personal morality.

After a little reflection on the origins of the campaign it is now obvious that no-one in Downing Street had thought beyond the first sound-bite or slogan. If they had, then they would have clearly realised what they were unleashing. Mercilessly and unrelentingly the focus turned on them; each and every human weakness and peccadillo was pounced upon.

David Porter has done a great service with this review of the current debate, and how it compares with past contributions on the theme from popular moral philosophers and theologians. As he points out, it was never even remotely plausible that public and private virtue could be shooed into separate, air-tight compartments. He says the public always have been, and always will bc, fascinated by the personal traits of their leaders. However he shows that despite the shallow rhetoric and the myth of a 1950's golden age of Mr Pastry, Listen with Mother and Happy Families, John Major did touch a deeper chord in the nation. Many ordinary people wished that the slogan could have meant more than the uncontentious ideas to which the campaign was reduced.

Back to Basics identifies why the campaign came unstuck so quickly. But it also offers a positive contribution, set in the context of biblical and contemporary Christian analysis, of how Christians committed to social change can provide content and meaning to the 'Back to Basics' ideal.

When the slogan was launched, it was coined to supersede

Lady Thatcher's jaded 'Victorian Values'. It sought to unite a bitterly divided party – licking its wounds after Maastricht – with a slogan which anyone from John Patten to Peter Lilley could fashion and use to mean whatever they wanted it to mean.

The phrase, like 'A Classless Society' before it, was elevated into tactics, a strategy, then a half-baked philosophy. But it threatened to engulf the entire administration. So what lessons can be drawn? If it is true that those who live by the sword die by it, politicians would be well-advised to refrain from scape-goating convenient groups of people. Single parents have been cruelly used by people who through a series of anti-family budget measures have added to the pressures on family life. This aspect has been part of an odious new agenda fashioned by the politics and economics of the American New Right. We in Britain have been mesmerised by every barmy idea from the voodoo economics of Milton Friedman to the propagandist harshness that blames victims in order to gain cheap support.

What has been missing so far in the 'Back to Basics' debate, and what David Porter provides in this book, is the balanced approach of Christian ethics. *Back to Basics* should encourage and prompt a moral climate where individuals will freely choose to pursue what the gospel demands. But it should also be about the pursuit by government of the goal of justice. The government's campaign will cease to fail when it begins to recognise the element of care and love bound up in a true morality. 'We will not have a moral society while people sleep on the streets, or while families are abandoned in a spiral of debt and poverty. But ultimately, we will not have a just society until both individuals and politicians take the basic step of going back to God, who is the source of hope, justice and love.

DAVID ALTON MP
MAY, 1994

PREFACE

This is a small book about a large subject, and I would like to begin with a few words about how it came to be written.

Back to Basics is the result of an invitation by OM Publishing to reflect on the current debate about basic values and the morality of political leadership. Those who are familiar with my other books will understand that the invitation was not issued because I am any kind of political expert or social analyst. Like the authors of a number of books that are quoted in the chapters that follow, I am a layman in these matters. Yet the issues that the book discusses are ones that have fascinated people for centuries, and not only political specialists. Few who read or study in any area, and fewer still who live as citizens of a society, escape them.

I have had two groups of people in mind as I have written this book. First are those of all faiths and none, who may be interested to know what a Christian opinion might be on the issues that currently dominate our headlines as I write, and which surface perennially in public discussion. I say 'a' Christian position rather than 'the' Christian position, for these are subjects on which Christians have not always agreed, as many of the following pages demonstrate. However, I have attempted to set out those elements on which there is considerable agreement among Christians, and where Christian morality may be said to have had an influence. In that sense, the book will I hope serve as an anthology, for a wide range of opinions are quoted – though the anthology, again, is not exhaustive. It's a personal selection that omits some significant people (for example Rienhold Niebuhr and R H Tawney among older writers and Ronald J Sider and Charles Colson among the more recent), and I have chosen those who are included not because they are definitive on the subject of Christianity and politics but because they seem to me to be saying important things on the particular issues of this book.

Secondly, I have had in mind those Christians who want to think through some of the issues from a biblical perspective, and who would then like some suggestions as to how faith can be translated into action. Christianity is a faith to change the world, and every believer is an agent for change to some degree or other.

I am rather afraid that both groups of readers will wish the book was longer. I hope nevertheless that it will be helpful as a stimulus, a contribution to the discussion, and a resource of ideas for further reading and action.

A number of friends and colleagues have discussed these matters with me over the years and I am grateful to them. No book of this nature is entirely its author's own, and I only hope that I have adequately acknowledged my sources in my footnotes. One friend who has been a particular help has been Peter Cousins, who has read the book as it progressed and made impartial and invaluable comments. This does not of course mean that he necessarily agrees with everything I have written, nor that he can be blamed for any shortcomings of the book.

Finally, may I make two apologies on editorial matters. First, for the exclusive and male-oriented vocabulary of many of the Christian writers from whom I quote. While one of the most heartening developments in Christian literature today is a move away from such language, it was not always so. I have resisted the temptation to silently alter such quotations. Fashions change, and while exclusive language sometimes strongly suggests a chauvinist frame of mind in the speaker, it is not necessarily the case. One of the worst offenders was Dorothy L Sayers, who is rightly recognised today as a powerful and witty champion of the rights of women.

Second, this book has a great many footnotes for its size. I hope that their usefulness will compensate for the clutter. As many of my quotations are intended to introduce readers to books rather than to embark on a thorough analysis of them, I thought it right to give as much help as possible in tracking my sources down.

DAVID PORTER

INTRODUCTION: BACK TO BASICS

We got talking at the check-out, watching the long queue of people ahead of us dumping groceries from heavily-laden trolleys on to the crowded supermarket counter.

'You'd think,' my neighbour said, 'that they'd get some more girls on the tills. Only four to deal with this lot, it's disgraceful.'

He had a point. The young woman cashier at our till was struggling with a bag of potatoes that had lost its price tag and looked about to split open. She probably wished they'd get some more girls on the tills too.

'Look at that,' he said, pointing at the next trolley but one. It was full of pre-packaged food, cake mixes, unappetising plastic cheese and white fluffy bread. 'Won't do anybody any good, that won't,' he said gloomily. 'You don't get food like you got when I was young. Bread you could taste, carrots with mud still on 'em.' He scanned the trolley again. 'Sugar Popsies,' he said distastefully. '*Yoghurt!*' The trolley's owner fortunately wasn't listening. I smiled apologetically to the queue in general. Nobody was listening anyway.

'But then,' he said, 'that's how it is nowadays.' The queue shuffled forward, he continued speaking. 'All downhill. Young people, they let them get away with anything. People sleeping together – can't leave your car anywhere – prices in the shops way up – kids swearing – sex on telly . . .'

The woman with the Popsies was now on her way out of the

supermarket door, and my neighbour was one position away from the till. He grabbed the 'next customer' marker, plonked it in place and began to get his shopping out of the trolley.

'What we want,' he said tersely, throwing the comment over his shoulder in my general direction, 'is a Return to Family Values. Stop the Rot. Get this Country Going Again.'

He began to argue with the assistant about the price of a large wholemeal loaf ('Added fibre for health, baked the old-fashioned way').

My grumpy acquaintance was by no means unique. Over the past decade or so, there has been a rising tide of discontent with what is usually called public morality; the way that we order our behaviour as a society.

Of course, it's not a modern complaint. Letters survive from classical antiquity, bewailing the fact that the young people of those days ran wild and lacked the sense of responsibility that previous generations possessed. It is a complaint that is part of that nostalgia for the past and distaste for the present which echoes through the centuries. Historian John Aubrey in the seventeenth century lamented the mindless destruction of antiquities; in the nineteenth century, Luddite manifestos bewailed the influx of new technologies and William Wordsworth complained to the newspapers that the opening of the proposed Rydal Railway would introduce insensitive people to an environment that had been enjoyed for generations by the sensitive and discriminating. Sociologist Raymond Williams has compiled an entertaining selection of such elegies for vanished golden ages, when things were not so unruly and dissolute. The nostalgia for the age of lost moral innocence is a theme repeated so far back in time, says Williams, that it probably looks back ultimately to the loss of Eden itself.[1]

But how golden was that golden age? Those who use the

1. Raymond Williams, *The Country and the City* (1973: Paladin edn 1975), ch 2.

past as a stick with which to beat the present tend to forget about such things as abject poverty, fatal epidemics, child slavery and much more. The most romantic of them wish that they had lived their lives out in one of the halcyon eras that they crave. Dornford Yates, a novelist who was romantic to the point of mindlessness, summarised the thought effectively in the words of one of his characters: 'Ah, to have died, full of years,' he sighed, 'in 1910!'

Many of those who long for a social moral renaissance felt distinctly cheered when in the winter of 1993/4 Prime Minister John Major coined the slogan 'Back to Basics'. It immediately conjured up the kind of values which people felt Major – perceived by many to be an essentially decent, if uncharismatic, figure – stood for. It offered appealing values: honesty, fidelity, respect, affection, compassion, mutual respect and integrity, in a celebration of a caring society and traditional family values.

The fact that it backfired quite so badly can be put down partly to extraordinary lack of forethought and partly to the fact that the more sensationalist media, fresh from royal muck-raking, naturally saw the new slogan as a gift. Lack of forethought there certainly was, for nobody seems to have remembered how badly Margaret Thatcher's call to return to 'Victorian Values' had rebounded upon her government (her opponents gleefully pointing to Victorian homelessness, Victorian vagrancy and a host of other Victorian Values that weren't in the government prospectus at all). And it is astonishing that nobody seems to have anticipated the enthusiasm with which elements of the media would scrutinise the private lives of government politicians. Though it was certainly true that a number of the stories that broke were particularly badly timed from the Government's point of view, most were the kind of story of which one might expect to find a few examples if the private lives of any group of several hundred individuals were raked over.

Thus a succession of prominent parliamentarians were exposed as morally fallible, in situations ranging from what seemed to be a tragic and lonely suicide to others which in happier times would not have been thought worth a fraction of the coverage they received. As ministers' sexual peccadilloes were made public, it was pointed out more than once that at the 1993 Conservative Party Conference the emphasis had been on traditional family values and that single parents had been selected for particular criticism; so what were members of the parliamentary Conservative party doing, fathering love-children, creating single-parent families, betraying their wives and wrecking their own families?

An embattled Prime Minister then explained that 'Back to Basics' was not about private and public morality after all, but about such 'basic values' as being able to read and write.

Yet many ordinary people wished that the slogan had, after all, meant more. The issues that had been raised were important ones, even though, as had happened in the royal scandal-stories of the previous eighteen months, the tabloids and some popular TV were presenting the parliamentary revelations more as entertainment than anything else. Questions were left unanswered. What is the proper relationship – if any – between private morality and public behaviour? Does it matter if somebody who is responsible for legislating the morality of the nation is himself or herself morally a mess? Is it really important if, as happens to be the case on the day that I am writing these words, the 'Minister responsible for Open Government' has declared that politics is more like poker than chess, and that there are occasions when it is necessary and acceptable to tell lies to the House of Commons?[2]

2. Statement made by Cabinet member William Waldegrave MP to the All-Party Treasury and Civil Service Committee, 8 March 1994. This comment, which was seized upon with gusto by opposition members, was defended by Mr Waldegrave, who clarified it by saying that he was referring only to statements about the devaluation of currency; the Labour Party spokesman on open government claimed that it would lead to a breakdown of public confidence in ministers.

Such questions prompted recollections of Watergate and the Profumo affair – the former more so, since America's President Clinton struggled in early 1994 with the repercussions of property dealings in which he and his wife had taken part. Both crises centred on the question: Are there higher standards of moral accountability for our leaders than for ourselves? Is it desirable that those who govern society should be morally without reproach? If we want a moral society, does that mean that we must therefore be governed by moral people?

The questions are all the more difficult because the moral climate is currently extremely ambivalent. A good example is the way that the popular media handled the allegations of marriage breakdown between the Prince and Princess of Wales. In the circulation wars raging in Fleet Street, papers competed to offer their readers more and more titillating 'evidence' – for example, tapes supposed to have been made of private conversations by both the Prince and the Princess, each talking to alleged lovers. The existence of the tapes was first announced as a matter of public interest; the heir to the throne, it was said, was making his wife desperately unhappy so that she was forced to seek consolation from male admirers (the 'Squidgy' tapes), and in addition that the Prince himself was having a liaison with another woman.

It appeared for a lengthy period that it was open season for hunting the entire Royal Family. Film of the Duchess of York on holiday in allegedly compromising circumstances with her financial advisor led to her very public disgrace. Every possible detail of the royal private lives came under scrutiny. Professional 'royal-watchers' appeared on television to pontificate about the state of the royal marriages, and to speculate on the likely future marriages and liaisons that might result; morning television discussion programmes and radio phone-ins invited members of the public to contribute their opinions.

The moral ambivalence lay in the way in which the matter was laid before us and how we were invited to respond to it. The down-market tabloids – especially those like the *Sun*, which seem to see themselves as the moral watchdogs of the royal family's activities while at the same time cultivating a breezy matiness (it was the *Sun* that coined the nickname 'Shy Di', for instance) – came out in favour of the Princess. Prince Charles was the cold, unfeeling husband unable to understand his wife or bond with his children. Here was an issue that seemed to be the departure point of the newspaper coverage: that we had the right to expect better of our leaders, that the man who would one day be king had let down his people by behaving badly (and later, when allegations of sexual impropriety with another woman were made, to have behaved immorally).

But much more prominence was given to the details of the marital breakdown than was needed to claim misbehaviour. It rapidly became clear that the tabloids, and one or two more up-market newspapers, were feeding a voyeuristic interest that may well have had an element of envy in it. Given that Princess Diana had a similar aura to that of a top model or Hollywood star, the whole story acquired overtones of a tawdry Hollywood soap. Moreover, the tabloids soon began to boast that in revealing details they were performing some kind of public moral service.

Certain central moral issues, however, were hardly ever addressed. For example, the titbits of scandal were often gained by immoral means; an obvious example being the retired executive who had invested in an expensive radio set, and proceeded to listen to a private conversation, record it and sell it to the newspapers. The action of the photographer who trespassed on the Duchess of York's holiday retreat and used a camera which was obviously designed to invade privacy was not much criticised either, least of all by the newspapers purchasing the right to print his pictures. An intriguing nexus of situational ethics and relative morals developed and quickly became hopelessly tangled.

The royal scandals of 1992/3 posed the issue of what we can expect of our leaders very well, especially as few newspaper omitted to draw the comparison between the antics of the younger royals and the exemplary life and conduct of the Queen. They also serve as a useful reminder of our second theme: the return to basic values. For behind the press coverage and the ballyhoo was a mystique that had died; the myth of the royal ideal moral family. In George V's time the Royal Family was projected and perceived as the ideal family, the family that was to be the model of the nation's families. The carefully-posed photographs and the formal appearances of its members contributed to an image of a moral, happy and united family unit. Many images of moral leadership crumbled in the post-war years, but the image of the perfect family at Buckingham Palace, Windsor and Sandringham survived longer than most and disintegrated all the more spectacularly in consequence. As the death of a popular myth, it was a loss both of a past golden age and of a particular political innocence.

This book is not primarily written as a response to the 'Back to Basics' initiative launched by the Conservative government, though I hope it will be a useful contribution to the debate. It is intended rather to be a discussion of the central questions that the initiative has, for many people, provoked; and it is an examination of what various people have had to say about them at various periods. Authorities mentioned go as far back as Plato; within the Christian church the range includes people as diverse as John Stott, William Temple, and C S Lewis.

I do not intend to draw from this wide range of authorities in order to create, piece by piece, a complex representation of the subject in all its aspects. That would require a much larger book. My approach, especially in Chapter Four, is borrowed from an idea in philosophy known as the 'essentially contested concept'[3]. There is much disagreement about

3. Cf. W B Gallie, *Philosophy and the Historical Understanding* (1964). I owe this reference to Bishop Stephen Sykes, *The Identity of Christianity* (SPCK, 1984), p 251 ff.

the 'essence' – the core meaning – of certain concepts and notions; the best way to arrive at the truth, it's argued, is to look not at what people agree that essence to be, but at their disagreements about it. I hope that by looking at the disagreements between those I quote, rather than at what they agree upon, the main strands of our subject will become clear.

The concept that is 'contested' in these pages has been succinctly summarised elsewhere by Raymond Johnston:

> [Public] policy is limited, if not determined, by what a nation believes on the whole to be right. Public morality is a shared system of moral ideals which guides conduct. Public as well as private behaviour is shaped by communally shared patterns of values. Public morality . . . is indicated 'officially' by the standards enshrined in the laws of the land, and by the codes of behaviour established for professions, trades and other groups. . . . It is also indicated by what people actually *do* to help or to harm, edify or destroy, their fellow citizens. . . . Thus public morality is both what [people] say they *ought* to do and also what they actually *do* do.[4]

This book is an attempt to explore the theme of public morality as interpreted by leaders and governors. Should we demand that those who wish us to behave as good people should themselves be good people? Should we indeed expect our leaders' faith, morals and conduct to reflect biblical standards? We shall be examining, too, the question of 'basic values'; is there a set of values to which all decent men and women should conform, and to which society should return as quickly as possible?

These are discussions that are particularly appropriate for the Christian community, which has a considerable stake

4. Raymond Johnston, *Caring and Campaigning* (Marshall Pickering, 1990), p 20–21.

in the morality debate and yet has historically often had a problem with the world of secular affairs.

Christians have traditionally held one of three broad positions, which may be summarised as follows:

The desert island option

Those holding to this position have argued that the world is fallen and that Christians ought to have no part in it. They shun secular entertainment, are suspicious of secular culture and have very few secular friends. Their theory is that because the world is destined for destruction, it is both sinful and wrong to become attached to it, so it is best rejected *in toto*. The most extreme representatives of the 'Desert Island' option reject newspapers, television and all secular mass media. Of what interest to a born-again, sanctified Christian are the doings of the fallen world? Professionally, such people prefer working in the healing and caring professions, or in manual work, where no great issues of secular compromise crop up.

It is a natural step then to argue that as one has no interest in the secular world, how it manages its affairs is entirely irrelevant. Believers live according to a different standard, the law of God. It is impossible for human laws, framed by fallen sinful human beings, adequately to reflect God's justice. In any case, those who administer such laws are themselves fallen and sinful. Among those who hold to this position, therefore, it is common to find those who refuse to vote, who object to a variety of laws and regulations on grounds of conscience, and are frequently involved in clashes – usually passive, non-violent ones – where their commitment to God's law has meant, for them, acting in civil disobedience.

What I am describing is, of course, at its most extreme what has been called Exclusivism, both as a formal denomination and also as a trend among many denominations (though Taylor Party Exclusivism proper has a second distinctive; a conviction that it is the only true biblical Christian church). Its central argument is based on a strong interpretation of several Bible verses, including 1 Corinthians 2:12, 'We have not received the spirit of the world but the Spirit who is from God, that we may understand what God has freely given us', and 1 John 2:15, 'Do not love the world or anything in the world. If anyone loves the world, the love of the Father is not in him.' Hence world-flight, the escape to a super-spiritual desert island in the middle of a twentieth-century sea of doubt, is seen as the best way of living as a Christian.

Although seen at its plainest in those denominations that have explicitly embraced it as an article of belief, exclusivism is to be found in most parts of the Christian church in varying degrees. Its main attraction is that to turn away from the laws and the jurisdiction of human beings is not to become lawless but to submit to a greater, divine, law; so it has inherent spiritual credentials (though even this cannot always be assumed, as can be seen for example in the heresy of antinomianism, where a conviction that one is irrevocably of God's Elect has led not only to lawlessness but also to immorality.)[5]

The biblical argument against this position has been developed, particularly in the last few decades, by writers on apologetics in many fields, such as C S Lewis, Lesslie Newbigin, Francis Schaeffer, Hans Rookmaaker and Os Guinness, and their books are well worth consulting. Their argument has been against what Kenneth Leech has called 'evangelical pietism', quoting Richard Zuercher:

> 'Salvation for evangelicals takes place in the realm of the cosmic spirits or in the inner realms of human conscience. Conversion happens when one claims to believe in Jesus's atonement and then feels forgiveness and inner peace.

5. The classic fictional text on antinomianism is the novel by James Hogg, *The Private Memoirs and Confessions of a Justified Sinner* (1824). Elsewhere in the present book I mention John Buchan's *Witch Wood* (p 72).

> Becoming a Christian is not seen to require any fundamental changes such as an acceptance of particular ways of behaving both inwardly and corporately that become an alternative to the broader society. One can become an evangelical Christian and still be a racialist, for example. . . .' By contrast, the new breed of evangelical places a more truly biblical emphasis on the Kingdom of God and on the social dimensions of salvation.[6]

But the argument that has greatest force is to be found in the words of Jesus himself in his last discourse to his disciples:

> I am coming to you now, but I say these things while I am still in the world, so that they may have the full measure of my joy within them. I have given them your word and the world has hated them, for they are not of the world any more than I am of the world. My prayer is not that you take them out of the world but that you protect them from the evil one. They are not of the world, even as I am not of it. Sanctify them by the truth; your word is truth. As you have sent me into the world, I have sent them into the world. For them I sanctify myself, that they too may be truly sanctified.
> (John 17:13–19)

The answer to the desert island case lies in the identification Jesus makes between himself and his disciples. For the Son of God, who came eating and drinking with sinners, visiting demoniacs and brilliantly crossing verbal swords with the intellectuals of his day, the desert island was simply not an option. Neither is it to be for the Christian.

The all-over tan option

The second position is perhaps even more extreme and is expressed something like this: 'I'm a Christian, and I know

6. Kenneth Leech quoting Richard Zuercher writing in *Third Way*: in, Leech, *The Social God* (SPCK, 1981), p 5.

that God is looking after me, and I know that in the end it's God who is running the world. So I'll simply live in the world like everybody else, I won't try to develop a "Christian perspective" on anything, least of all politics, because God will see everything all right in the end.'

Those holding this position would reject the idea of Christian schools, Christian media and Christian political parties (all often proposed to various degrees by those arguing for a Desert Island approach). They don't see the need for them. Christianity is a personal, private, spiritual matter; it has little to do with the nitty-gritty of everyday life. But that doesn't mean that the world need be shunned. Certainly it is a godless, immoral place – but never mind! We can jump in at the deep end because God himself is our supreme life-belt.

Those who argue like this tend not to lean as heavily on biblical support as do the Desert Island party, for there are not many verses that even appear to support their case. They argue rather from general principles and logical deduction, to show that one need not count the risks if one's God is omnipotent. However, the Bible refuses to endorse their position, most notably in the Gospel account of Jesus', life when he is subjected to precisely the same temptation:

> Then the devil took him to the holy city and had him stand on the highest point of the temple. 'If you are the Son of God,' he said, 'throw yourself down. For it is written:
>
> "He will command his angels concerning you,
> and they will lift you up in their hands,
> so that you will not strike your foot against a stone." '
>
> Jesus answered him, 'It is also written: "Do not put the Lord your God to the test." '
> (Matthew 4:5–7)

If Jesus declined to leap into danger relying on God to save him miraculously, then his followers must likewise decline to do so.

The third way

The third option can be described simply as the biblical third way: avoiding the extremes of total world-flight and total world-embrace, it seeks to navigate a course that is determined by a biblical approach and a biblical understanding.

Of course it is a difficult option, much more difficult to apply than either of those described above. It calls for continual reflection on the spiritual and moral dimensions of the everyday. But that does not mean cultivating a morbid spirituality that is suspicious of everything, that trusts nothing and enjoys even less. It means that we should consider as a basic element of spiritual maturity that perception which the Bible calls 'the mind of Christ'. Thus Paul urges his Roman readers:

> Therefore, I urge you, brothers, in view of God's mercy, to offer your bodies as living sacrifices, holy and pleasing to God – this is your spiritual act of worship. Do not conform any longer to the pattern of this world, but be transformed by the renewing of your mind. Then you will be able to test and approve what God's will is – his good, pleasing and perfect will. (Romans 12:1–2)

The progression is clear: first the offering of self, then the renewal of the mind, then, as the culmination of the process, the ability to test and approve what God's will is. In other words, the Christian mind is the way to Christian maturity, not an optional extra for those of an academic bent.

The owner of a Christian mind will want to ask questions about the society in which he or she lives. What kind of society is pleasing to God? What kind of society will best enshrine the principles of justice, compassion and generosity which God seems to consider such vital issues? How can we 'let justice roll on like a river' (Amos 5:24)? To what extent are we responsible as a society for the decisions our governments take? To what extent should we be concerned about the moral standards of our nation? And to what extent should we be concerned that those who lead our society should live moral lives? The very questions, indeed, that this book sets out to examine; questions that many Christians have asked, like David Alton MP: 'What kind of country?'[7], Francis Schaeffer: 'How should we then live?'[8], and Lesslie Newbigin: 'What is Christ's relationship to the principalities and powers?'.[9]

The argument of the third way claims that these are legitimate questions for Christians to ask and that a biblical Christianity will inevitably ask them. We shall look at some of them in the chapters that follow, though in a book of only 40,000 words it will not be possible to do more than suggest directions for more extended thinking.

We begin the discussion at an earlier point, however. In Chapter One we examine the concept of a Christian society, and we start with the notion, often proposed, of that society in its most explicit form: a Christian utopia. If that is achievable, then the questions become very simple, for all our leaders will be, if not priests, then certainly people of faith; and if they do not behave as such, they can rightfully be thrown out of office.

7. David Alton, *What Kind of Country?* (Marshall Pickering, 1988).
8. Francis Schaeffer, *How Should We Then Live?* (Fleming H Revell, 1976).
9. The question posed on p 207 of Lesslie Newbigin, *The Gospel in a Pluralist Society* (SPCK, 1989).

1

A CHRISTIAN SOCIETY

It seemed to him as he kneeled he began to pray, and the vision was more of a longing for a future than a reality in the future. The Church of Jesus in the city and throughout the country! Would it follow Jesus? Was the movement begun in Raymond to spend itself in a few churches . . . and then die away as a local movement, a stirring on the surface, but not to extend deep and far? He felt with agony after the vision again. He thought he saw the Church of Jesus in America open its heart to the moving of the Spirit, and rise to the sacrifice of its ease and self-satisfaction, in the name of Jesus. He thought he saw the motto, 'What would Jesus do?' inscribed over every church door, and written on every church member's heart. (*Charles M Sheldon*)[10]

In the Parliamentary galleries I meet the head of the Christian Labor Association of North America, the international association of Christ-believing workers. I leave the gallery and pick up a copy of *Voice*, the Christian daily newspaper, and thank God for the headline which reads 'Government monopoly in education ends' . . . I stroll

10. Charles M Sheldon, *In His Steps* (Henry E Walter, 1948), p 236.

> along Bank Street toward the news stand to pick up a copy of *Meaning*, the Christian weekly which has replaced *Playboy* as the top circulation North American magazine. . . . I take a deep, clean breath. My heart is full of joy, for America is [now] a good place to live, a free place, free for all people to live out of their convictions. It is a place where God's name is honored and revered for His people are honest, open, good representatives of Christ. . . . And I reflect back on all those who said, 'It can't be done. It's too idealistic. We'll never make it.' (*James A Olthuis*)[11]

The first quotation is from a best-selling novel by Charles Sheldon, *In His Steps*, which almost half a century ago provided an immensely popular vision of a society profoundly affected by Christian values; a revival not so much in terms of repentance and conversion, but in the working out by the church, in ethical and social terms, of the character and teachings of Jesus. The second quotation is from a vision presented by James Olthuis as a challenge to the Christian church to work and pray; it is a vision of a nation benignly governed by Christian values and Christian politicians.

It's a fascinating thought. What might a moral or even a Christian society be expected to look like?

No king but Christ

For some the only society that deserves the title 'Christian' is one in which Christ is, quite literally, king and ruling through his regents, such as is implied in the quotation from James Olthuis: that is, a Christian utopia. In such a society, everybody would go to church, and all families would bring up their children as practising Christians. All the schools

11. John A Olthuis, 'The Wages of Change' in: Olthius et al, *Out of Concern for the Church* (Wedge, 1970), pp 20, 21.

would teach Christian doctrine, all behaviour and morals would be determined by Christian ethics, and in any matter that required arbitration or resolution the Bible would be taken as the unquestioned rule and regulation of law. Those who governed such a society would be whole-heartedly Christian believers, and such a faith-commitment would be an inescapable qualification for any office in government or the legislature. In many people's ideal Christian state, any social unit, structure or programme that did not expressly hold to a full Christian basis would be outlawed and the law would include a range of proscriptions and measures to punish non-Christianity.

There have, of course, been many attempts to bring such a 'Christian state' into existence.

Conversion by force

Some attempts have been backed by force, both political and military. Among the crudest on record is the version of the attempted conversion of Iceland in AD 997 narrated by Snorri Sturluson in his chronicle history, *Heimskringla*:

> When King Olaf Trygvesson had been two years king of Norway, there was a Saxon priest in his house who was called Thangbrand, a passionate, ungovernable man, and a great man-slayer; but he was a good scholar, and a clever man. The king would not have him in his house on account of his misdeeds; but gave him the errand to go to Iceland, and bring that land to the Christian faith. . . . Thangbrand was two years in Iceland, and was the death of three men before he left it.[12]

Thangbrand's evangelistic methods included intimidation, torture and murder; it is something of a relief, after this sometimes unreliable chronicler, to read another version of

12. Snorri Sturluson, *Heimskringla: Part One, The Olaf Sagas*, c1220: trs Samuel Laing, rev Jacqueline Simpson. Vol 1 (Dent, rev edn 1964), p 65.

the process. Stephen Neill observes that 'Iceland is the one country of those times in which Christianity was accepted by genuinely democratic process'[13] – a process completed in AD 1016.

But enough survives in the literature of Iceland to indicate that if Sturluson was guilty of exaggeration, he was still reflecting some historical reality. And of course a conversion initiated in this way will not lead to the spiritual rebirth of a whole people. Some Icelanders converted to Christianity out of fear, some out of necessity, and some hoped for practical benefits (as elsewhere in Europe, it was a great period of church building, for benefactors of the church often expected something in return in the after-life). And many, officially embracing the new faith, continued quietly to practise the beliefs and ethos of the old – which, again, was not a uniquely Icelandic phenomenon.

The subsequent history of Iceland was one on which paganism and Christianity continued to sit uneasily together; the gripping *Njal's Saga*[14] is a vivid portrayal of a society in which the two religious ideologies clash. Whatever else mediaeval Iceland was, it was not a 'Christian society' in the sense of a society operating by universal Christian consensus.

Similar in some ways is the rise of Oliver Cromwell, the English Puritan, leading to the execution of Charles I and the proclamation of Cromwell as Lord Protector in 1653, thereby bringing the political leadership of Britain under a version of theocratic rule. Cromwell did not come to power out of a desire for wealth or position; he had both already. His dispute with the king was an irreconcilable clash between two theories of government, religiously profoundly different, and it was Cromwell who won by a military victory.

13. Stephen Neill, *A History of Christian Missions* (Pelican History of the Church vol 6, 1964), p 106.
14. The Penguin translation (1960) is excellent, but a brilliantly idiomatic version is Henry Treece, *The Burning of Njal* (Bodley Head, 1964).

It was a victory hedged by constraints, and relationships between the Protector and the Council of State and later the Parliament were difficult. Cromwell's interregnum was marked by several acts of draconian strength; following the execution of the king, the army was the effective instrument of authority in England and the nation was essentially a military dictatorship. Yet Cromwell's achievement was to turn his militarily secured position into what was really England's first constitutional monarchy. Assessments of Cromwell vary, but most record the tolerant attitude resulting from his desire for 'liberty for tender consciences', and his lack of interest in founding a dynasty or holding power for its own sake. There is no doubt that for 'papists or prelates' living in Cromwell's England, liberty was only partial; and Parliament, with its wealth qualification, was far from modern democracy in action. Yet Christopher Hill, who was hardly in agreement with Cromwell's religion, concludes a study of the Protector (after emphasising that opinions vary greatly) like this:

> So long as men and women 'with the root of the matter in them' call in question those values of their society which deny our common humanity, so long indeed as the great issues of liberty and equality which Oliver raised remain unresolved, so long will he continue to fascinate, and the debate over him will continue.[15]

Cromwell's vision of what England should be is sometimes difficult to determine, but it does not seem to envisage a nation in which Christianity would be enforced by law to the extent of criminalising non-Christians. Had the Protectorate survived Oliver's lack of interest in his own succession, it would have been a remarkable England, but certainly not a Christian utopia. If tolerance is a Christian virtue, perhaps he was too much of a Christian to enforce a Christian state,

15. Christopher Hill, *God's Englishman: Oliver Cromwell and the English Revolution* (1970: Penguin edn 1972), pp 266–7.

if that meant depriving those who disagreed with him of civil and human rights.

Examples could be multiplied of societies in which Christianity has been imposed by force or by decree. Often the societies that result have qualities deriving directly from Christian ethics and morality; sometimes the reverse; sometimes little changes at all. It should be clear, however, that whatever else a forced national conversion achieves it does not produce a society of Bible-believing Christians, all without exception loving God with all their heart and soul and might.

Spiritual awakenings

However, Christian nations may also come into being because of wide-ranging spiritual movements.

Virtually ignored by the Christian and secular media today, two states in modern India are almost wholly Christian. Of the 686,000 people in Mizoram, which neighbours Bangladesh, 85% are Christians – almost the whole indigenous population.[16] The first Western missionaries arrived 150 years ago, but were banned after Independence in 1947. The Christian community at that time was considerably less than 50% of the population, but took up the task of evangelisation and completed it. Now no other nation on earth has sent out a higher proportion of its population as Christian missionaries.

Nagaland (population 1,218,000) bordering Burma is the world's only Baptist state: it too has an 85% Christian population, and of the indigenous Naga tribes people almost every one is a Christian. In the middle of the nineteenth century the Nagas were head-hunters, but the first converts came following evangelism that began in 1860 by the American Baptist Missionary Societies. The Western missionaries

16. Statistics are taken from Patrick Johnstone, *Operation World* (OM Publishing, 5th edn, 1993).

were forced to leave in the same way as those in Mizoram were, and the indigenous Naga church likewise finished their task. Today, Naga believers are committed to world-wide evangelism, and a number of major missionary organisations in the subcontinent recruit workers from the Nagas.

On hearing of Mizoram and Nagaland a likely reaction (following disbelief that the Christian media have told us so little about them) is to speculate what life must be like in a state with an almost entirely Christian population, and to ask what lessons might be learned in terms of public morality and government criteria. But the situation in both states is that the majority religion is one not favoured by the Indian majority leadership. India, the world's largest functioning democracy, is a union of member states and a confessedly secular society. But discrimination against both Christians and Muslims is growing, and the surging political strength of neo-Hinduism has led to some anti-conversion laws. Though the fruit of 200 years of missionary and indigenous Christian work in India is plain to see, the Christian majorities of Mizoram and Nagaland belong to a political union in which the official estimate of the Christian population is 2.61% and unofficial estimates place it at no more than 4%.

Mizoram and Nagaland are extraordinary stories of the power of the gospel (and vindications of the sacrificial, ground-breaking missionary work done in the generations since William Carey first visited India), but they do not constitute theoretical models of Christian states. In both, the prevailing spirituality is somewhat pietistic, and most Christians simply do not see a relationship between their faith and their politics. In the wider Indian context, to be a Christian is to invite hardship and oppression, for those who have the absolute power of government are secular authorities. In Nagaland especially, the remoteness of the region has cut the people off from the world-wide church, and the history of Nagaland's struggle for independence over decades[17] has led to a highly volatile political situation; today the state is virtually closed, and access is almost impossible.

The analogy of Islam

Those who cherish the idea of a state run by Christians, in which the Bible is the law and the measure of citizenship is Christian behaviour and ethics, might consider the example of the fundamentalist Islamic states, where precisely this basis applies, but in terms of Islam and the *Shari'a* law.

> The Shari'a (Islamic law) is much more than a legal system or a code of practice. It originates from none other than God himself. It is based directly on the commandments concerning religious duties found in the Qur'an. . . . In addition, the detailed laws concerning the conduct of day to day living are based on the example of the Prophet Muhammad, as revealed to him and practised by him.[18]

In fundamentalist Islamic states, the rulers are clergy and the morals and ethics of the people are bound by the word of Allah as revealed in the Qur'an and the Hadith.

At first sight this might seem to be an enviable system, to which Christians ought to aspire. But there are several reasons why the Islamic system could not be applied to Christianity. One is that Islam does not permit *freedom of conscience* and does not tolerate dissent. The penalties of Islam are severe, and are an exact religious retribution. Most notorious is the case of Salman Rushdie, though few understand the reasons why orthodox Muslims found *The Satanic Verses* offensive (those reasons are well explained in

17. A deeply informed European view of the situation in the Indian 'buffer states' is to be found in the work of George Patterson over many years, eg *A Fool at Forty* (Word, 1970).
18. Ron George, 'Islamic Law' in: Anne Cooper (comp), *Ishmael My Brother* (MARC/EMA, 1993), p 129.

the symposium by Anne Cooper from which I quoted above). The Ayatollah's *fatwa* is irreversible; Rushdie's crime against Islam can be dealt with only by the execution of the offender. International representation, diplomatic bargaining and such political pressure as has been exerted have all had no effect. But liberty of conscience is a specifically Christian concept, and while one might expect a Christian administration to enact laws to punish blasphemy, the biblical understanding of forgiveness differs radically from the Islamic concept.

Another reason why a Christian equivalent of a fundamentalist Islamic state would not work *is the biblical understanding of civil law*. The Bible contains substantial legal codes, but the Christian gospel does not assume that these will be enacted in their original forms. Many were made to separate God's people from cultic practices that no longer apply – hence the prohibition on trimming the corners of beards. Many Old Testament laws had to do with hygiene in a nomadic desert situation. Others refer to slavery, now no longer a common practice. Still more are concessions to prevailing culture, such as the law on divorce, but their status is qualified in other parts of the Bible – in the case of the Mosaic teaching on divorce, in Jesus' words: 'Moses permitted you to divorce your wives because your hearts were hard. But it was not this way from the beginning' (Matthew 19:8).

In some areas the interpretation of the biblical civil law is difficult, as for example with the prohibitions on homosexuality, the subject of fierce and continuing debate. But it is at any rate clear that what the Bible provides is not a legal system that can be applied to modern situations, but the working out of a legal code, in one cultural situation at one time, on the basis of the unchangeable attributes and character of God. Of course many of those laws will still be perfectly applicable today. But for many others, the task of biblical law makers today is to consider what principles under-girded the Mosaic law and then to apply them to modern situations.

The Islamic interpretation of Qur'anic law sometimes encounters similar areas of disagreement and context. In Islam, the problem is solved by the principles of agreement and analogy, whereby if a majority of teachers concur about the meaning of a scripture, or if an acceptable analogy can be drawn, this becomes the law. But this presupposes a government by clergy which is quite outside the Judaeo-Christian tradition and at odds with constitutional monarchy, republicanism and parliamentary democracy. A Christian state on Islamic lines would consequently have to adopt such an autocratic leadership that the Christian principle of liberty of conscience (one dear to Oliver Cromwell's heart, among others) would have to be sacrificed.

A third point that must be made about the fundamentalist Islamic state is that *it is not universally honoured by its citizens.* While stories of wealthy Muslims travelling to the West to enjoy the decadence denied them at home are often scurrilous invention, there is no indication that in the Islamic states the population as a whole consents to be governed in that there is a universal commitment of the heart and will to the government as regents of God. There are plenty of examples of insurrection and rebellion, of leaders deposed by their people on grounds other than that they were failing as Muslims, of divisions and breakdowns within Islam itself and within countries. In this Islam is no different or worse than any other human community. It does mean, however, that the fundamentalist Islamic state, despite its confessed dependence on God and the Islamic scriptures, does not provide a conspicuously good model of what an equivalent Christian state might be.

The limitations of theocracy

When Christians see a past or present nation or state, populated or governed by committed Christians whether by force or by consent, it is difficult not to reflect on the possibility of a theocracy, a society run on God's terms and moderated by God's laws, like the Old Testament Israel. But a revival of theocracy is an unrealistic hope, and, it might be argued, an unbiblical one.

It is unrealistic because in most cases *it seeks to impose the rule of God by law.* Gordon Spykman tells the following story:

> A friend of mine . . . studying at Berkeley a dozen years ago during the height of the counter-culture 'revolution' tells about a discussion of politics in which he became involved. Very quickly the others detected in his ideas a different perspective. They challenged him, 'Who are you anyway?' 'I'm a Christian,' he replied. 'A Christian! You Christians have had your chance since 313.[19] Now it's our turn.' They were referring to this long-lived assumption that society as a whole could be Christianized, and that Christianity could be imposed by the sword or by papal edict upon all people. That is not what we ought to mean by Christian politics.[20]

To follow Christ requires the commitment of heart and will. Neither can be made captive by force, only won by consent; and the law of love is not enforceable by fear. The vision of a Christian utopia generally consists of an attempt to create the kingdom of God as a visible human political and social organisation. John Stott points out the error:

> The Kingdom of God is not Christianized society. It is the divine rule in the lives of those who acknowledge Christ. It has to be 'received', 'entered' or 'inherited', he said, by humble and penitent faith in him. And without a new birth it is impossible to see it, let alone enter it.

19. The reference is to the official recognition of Christianity in AD 312–313 by the Roman emperor Constantine I. Ironically, Constantine's own conversion is debatable. See eg Gerald Bray, *Creeds, Councils and Christ* (IVP, 1984), pp 124ff.
20. Gordon Spykman, 'Beyond Words to Action' in: James W Skillen, ed, *Confessing Christ and Doing Politics* (Assoc for Public Justice Education Fund, Washington USA, 1982), p 30.

> Those who do receive it like a child, however, find themselves members of a new community of the Messiah, which is called to exhibit the ideals of his rule in the world and so to present the world with an alternative social reality.[21]

It comes as a gift, not by decree; it cannot be legislated for.

The notion of theocratic utopia is unrealistic, too, because *it involves a confusion of categories.* It implies that one of the tasks appointed to the Church of Christ on earth is to govern. But the church is not the state, any more than it is the school or the family. Nor is it ever implied in the Bible that the Christian's highest moral rule is to be that of the laws of the country in which he or she lives; there is a still higher moral law in existence and it is to that law that a Christian is first obligated. No state legislature can replace it, nor is it the proper task of the state to do so. Which is not to say that the two moral laws, that of church and that of state, are irrelevant to each other, as we shall see. But the two cities identified by St Augustine – 'two societies of human beings, one of which is predestined to reign with God from all eternity, the other doomed to undergo eternal punishment with the devil'[22] – continue with different agendas. The business of the church, argued Peter Baelz, lies in 'a willingness to respond to the way of our Lord whatever the consequences and not to believe that it is the duty of the Christian Church to manage the affairs of the world'.[23]

There is a third reason why the desire for a 'Christian state' is unrealistic: *it fails to acknowledge the richness and complexity of Christian diversity.* It supposes that there is a

21. John Stott, *Issues Facing Christians Today* (Marshalls, 1984), p 7. Stott's chapter on 'Involvement' is particularly helpful in this discussion.
22. Augustine, *The City of God*, xv.1. See p 86 in the present book for further reference to Augustine.
23. Contribution to *The Church and the Bomb*, General Synod debate, February 1983.

single Christian position – even a Christian consensus – on all the issues on which a state might legislate or make moral pronouncements. But once one has moved away from the propositional, credal core of the Christian gospel (the central doctrines that might be summed up in one of the historic creeds or the statement of basis of faith of a modern Christian organisation), there is often no such consensus. It is the consequence of how the Scriptures are written. The Bible is not a compendium of systematic theology, neatly arranged with headings and subheadings. It is a mixture of narrative, poetry and discourse (this fact does not compromise at all any doctrine of full verbal inspiration of Scripture). This anthology of 66 books was the vehicle God chose to reveal himself, through the inspiration of the Holy Spirit, to humanity. It speaks infallible truth, but in many areas there has historically been disagreement as to what that truth is.

Consequently a wide range of ethical and moral issues, for example – the very areas in which governments make laws – cannot be resolved by a commonly-agreed reading of the Bible. The issue of war and peace is one. Arguments on both sides are defended by a wealth of biblical quotation, but there remain two sides. Where there is genuine disagreement among Christians, to make one side or other into constitutional law would make those who hold the other view criminals – as has often been the position of pacifists in Western democracies. Rejecting the option of 'Christian government' in this sense, Bernard Thorogood comments:

> Today there is still not one prescription for a Christian regime or a Christian economy. The many-voiced jury is here to stay. We are better not to have a Christian political party, for that assumes there is one Christian answer to the myriad questions confronting society.[24]

24. Bernard Thorogood, *Judging Caesar* (United Reformed Church, 1990), p 126.

The difficulty is a huge one, for it is not a matter of identifying and espousing the truth of one issue, but of the whole gamut of moral issues. A Christian government taking power on such a basis would rapidly find that numerous Christians, who agreed on a majority of their government's rulings, parted company on one or two. Not only would such a government have a secular, 'official' opposition, it would have one or more Christian groups opposed to at least some of its actions.

The problem is demonstrated by the present-day growth of 'single issue politics', in which Christians urge other Christians to vote for a party or a leader on the grounds that on a particular issue important to them, the candidate is satisfactorily biblical. Thus, for example, pro-life candidates are endorsed by anti-abortion groups. The inadequacy of this approach is that it ignores what the totality of an effective candidate is. I once watched a candidate grilled by a Christian audience, and observed the general dissatisfaction when the candidate refused to commit himself on the issue of abortion. My feeling was one of great relief, for the candidate was clearly out of touch with the constituency he planned to represent, inadequately briefed, and inexpert in most of the matters on which he was questioned. Had he committed himself to a pro-life position, he would have been assured – to judge from the conversations I heard afterwards – of the votes of a large number of Christians present. I hold a strong pro-life position myself, but I want my elected representatives to be competent at their job; in any case, a candidate being embraced by the pro-life lobby might at the same time be rejected by the pacifist lobby, or the anti-Sunday-Trading lobby, or any of many other Christian pressure groups – so the Christian vote, if organised on single issues, would inevitably be split.

A fourth reason why the quest for a Christian utopia is unrealistic is that *it ignores the offence of the cross.* At the heart of the Christian gospel is a truth unacceptable to people who are not Christians: that there is no absolute merit in human effort, or in human nobility, or in human good intentions; that God sees everybody as equally fallen, that there is nothing in us to commend us to him, and that the only way to be right with our Maker is to bow to a crucified criminal who died an ignominious death on a cross. Such a faith will never command national adherence, for politics is the art of the possible, and gospel truth is not negotiable. The vision of James Olthuis quoted at the beginning of this chapter communicates a society in which the church commands universal affection and respect, and suggests that if one prays hard enough and works hard enough, it is possible to make it happen. Such a prospect is certainly promised in Scripture. It is the hope of the world according to the prophets, a vision that will become reality after the return of Jesus Christ; whether we may expect its earlier implementation in history is much less certain.

The Christian influence on society

If it is true, as I have suggested so far, that the hope of an earthly Christian society – in the sense of one governed by a Christian consensus, with Christian values and morals written into the code of law – cannot be realised, does this mean that the church and state are doomed to travel on parallel lines, aware of each other's existence but mutually irrelevant?

The Bible itself makes it very clear that this is not to be; that not only does the church need the state for its civil provisions and protections, but the state needs the church. The church provides a symbolic pattern of government:

> [The question is] whether there is any way in which we can understand the form of our society so as to give us a new orientation and a new impetus . . . Are there any symbols of hope, symbols of community, symbols of individuality-in-community, which transcend both the system of a warring conflict of interests and the system of central

planning of society by the state? Are there here any resources of hope?[25]

Such a symbolic pattern of government can be seen in various contexts. It is not by chance, for example, that in several Eastern European countries at present the church is recognised as one of the few trustworthy agencies of social welfare. In Ethiopia and in what was Yugoslavia, Christian aid organisations have several times been the only ones officially endorsed by the Ethiopian government and by the Red Cross respectively.

The gospel is a mandate for social care, and as such often stands in rebuke to the secular state (and to the church, where this necessary aspect of Christianity has been neglected). The same is true in other areas. The eighteenth-century Evangelical revival in England was not just a spiritual revival but a revival of literacy. Spiritual awakenings are commonly linked to social reform beyond the expected drop in crime. In America, revival has sometimes led to the initiation of fairer business practices.

Many great social reformers drew their inspiration from their Christian faith. Not all pioneering work by missionaries in medicine and education has been tied to evangelism. In contrast to several of the cults, few Christian aid organisations currently working in famine and other disaster spots demand a Christian commitment as a condition of receiving aid. Historically, Western society was changed radically by the work of Shaftesbury and of Wilberforce. There are many more examples that could be cited. All provide symbolic patterns of government.

25. Peter Baelz, 'The ethics of Strikes in the Caring Professions', *Crucible* Oct-Dec 1975, quoted in an essay by Daniel Hardy in D W Hardy and P H Sedgwick, *The Weight of Glory . . . the Future of Liberal Theology* (T & T Clark, 1991), p 131. Hardy goes on to make the point that the pattern must not remain merely symbolic but must be interpreted in structural and formal patterns of church government.

When Jesus required his audience to give to Caesar what was Caesar's and to God what was God's, he was not suggesting that the two sets of accounts had nothing to do with each other. One obvious example where they do relate is that of the evil government that perpetrates laws and enactments which godly people have no choice but to oppose. Civil disobedience is something that Christians have always adopted as a method of engaging with a godless authority. An outstanding example of Christian defiance of an evil government, where disobedience was forced to turn into violent opposition, is that of Dietrich Bonhoeffer, executed in April 1945 on a charge of treason. He had been working with Resistance fighters and was involved in plotting to kill Hitler. For Bonhoeffer, Hitler's edicts and the Nazification of the German church were such grave matters that disobedience was not enough. The strongest possible action was justified. As a Christian, he considered the interests of his Lord and his church to be directly threatened by the Nazi regime.

This does not contradict the point made earlier, that the church is not the state and must not invade that sphere of operation that is the state's proper function. But neither can Bonhoeffer's action be contradicted by appealing to those who argue for the privatisation of religion, saying that the church ought to concentrate on what it is good at – prayer, worship, evangelism, administering the sacraments, etc. – and let the state get on with the business of government (a suggestion often made by governments who find themselves publicly rebuked by Christian spokespersons).

The privatisation argument has been well expressed by Rachel Tingle, who selects a number of targets in her study *Another Gospel?* – perhaps too many, for it is sometimes difficult to separate the strands of her discussion. She quotes with approval William Temple who, 'in his later years at least, went to some pains to draw a distinction between individual Christian political action and corporate Church engagement',[26] and contrasts it with 'the present situation in the Church of England' which she summarises thus: 'From about the mid–1970s onwards, the involvement of the Church in secular political issues has become a mainstream activity with official backing and considerable resources devoted to it.'[27]

Rachel Tingle certainly does not disparage Christian social concern and she allows a significant role in the Anglican Church for such bodies as the Board for Social Responsibility. But she warns against a defined church political agenda, making the necessary point that it is all too possible for churches to acquire a particular political complexion or label. The church, she appears to argue, can and should act as a critique of the secular government through individual members, but this is not a task for the church as a whole.

It is an argument that is complex and deserves thorough dialogue. But Bonhoeffer, who fought against his own church's failure to critique a godless regime with a corporate biblical voice, was careful not to restrict this response to the individual level:

> The Bible does not recognise our distinction between the outward and the inward . . . I want to start from the premise that God shouldn't be smuggled into some last secret place, but that we should frankly recognise that the world, and people, have come of age, that we shouldn't run man down in his worldliness, but confront him with God at his strongest point, that we should give up all our clerical tricks, and not regard psychotherapy and existentialist philosophy as God's pioneers . . . The Word of God

26. Rachel Tingle, *Another Gospel? An Account of the Growing Involvement of the Anglican Church in Secular Politics* (Christian Studies Centre, 1988), p 15.
27. Ibid, p 16.

> is far removed from this revolt from below. On the contrary, it reigns.[28]

The gospel transforms not only individual Christians but the whole society in which individuals live. Christ did not come to redeem a holy huddle but to redeem human kind. A Christianity that remains within cloisters and does not make an impact on society is only a partial Christianity. That is the burden of the last words of Jesus to his disciples: Go into the world and make a difference. And they did, for in the space of a few years the world was turned upside down – not by a conglomeration of concerned individuals, but by the rising power of the young church of Christ.

One of the most interesting phenomena in recent years of church growth has been the proliferation of Christian organisations dedicated to exploring and promoting the relevance of the Christian gospel and of the Bible to the issues of the modern world. Organisations such as L'Abri Fellowship, Christian Impact, the *Gospel and Our Culture* project, the Arts Centre Group, the Evangelical Alliance, CARE Trust, the Jubilee Centre . . . it is a long list. It is interesting, too, that almost all have a completely orthodox, biblical basis of faith. This is not a movement of a new Christian cult. It is a (perhaps long overdue) expression of the Christian conviction that truth makes a difference, that the Bible has something to say to society, that government and social change are among many matters to which the Christian church neither can nor should remain indifferent.

In introducing a major study of this subject and of Christianity as contemporary faith, John Stott sets out the issues sharply:

> Can the gospel really be 'modernized'? Is it feasible to expect the church to apply the historic faith to the con-

28. Letter to Eberhard Bethge quoted in: Edwin Robertson, *The Shame and the Sacrifice: the Life and Preaching of Dietrich Bonhoeffer* (Hodder & Stoughton, 1987), p 257.

> temporary scene, the Word to the world, without either betraying the former or alienating the latter? Can Christianity retain its authentic identity and demonstrate its relevance at the same time, or must one of these be sacrificed to the other? Are we obliged to choose between retreating into the past and making a fetish of the present, between reciting old truths which are stale and inventing new notions which are spurious? Perhaps the greater of these two dangers is that the church will attempt to recast the faith in such a way as to undermine its integrity and render it unrecognizable to its original heralds.[29]

Augustine's two cities remain, but not in isolation nor as parallel, mutually exclusive. Christians are called to be in the world. Our calling to live in that reality is validated by nothing less than the words of Jesus himself, in his prayer for all disciples past and present, in the Gospel of John:

> My prayer is not that you take them out of the world but that you protect them from the evil one. They are not of the world, even as I am not of it. Sanctify them by the truth; your word is truth. As you sent me into the world, I have sent them into the world. For them I sanctify myself, that they too may be truly sanctified (John 17:15–19).

The church is, to use the biblical phrase, to be salt and light in the world. Its light is to shine before men and women, displaying what John Stott describes above as an 'alternative social reality'. Christians are to be so different that the difference intrigues and confronts secular people. That is the calling to individual Christians, whether on the domestic, business or national level. But the church as a whole has a commission too, and that commission does not involve only the areas of worship, ecclesiology, Bible study and pastoral counselling. It involves that interface with the world, that

29. John Stott, *The Contemporary Christian* (IVP, 1992), pp 17–18.

dialogue with Caesar, that has been a part of living in the world since the church began.

The Christian claim upon the state

We are left with one question more before we move on.

If the church and state are not mutually exclusive, but each has to do with the other; if, just as the state has a religious policy, so the church must decide what its attitude to the secular powers must be – what demands can and should the church make of society?

The church exists as a critique of the world. Its very presence among human structures incarnates Jesus Christ by whom all earthly powers will be judged. Christians are obligated to cultivate the mind of Christ, and with that mind to test everything, not merely a sacred subset of the wider world.

The question of what expectations and criteria the church is entitled (or indeed commanded) to apply is one that has received a wide range of answers. To some of these we turn in our next chapter.

2

REBUKING POLITICIANS

Getting the facts right

In one situation at least the Church has a clear right to critique politicians: that is, when politicians offer definitions of what Christianity is or what the Bible teaches. In such cases, politics has ventured into the legitimate province of the church; and it becomes the job of the church to make sure that the politicians get it right.

Misunderstanding Christianity

This is an issue that is not confined to politics. For example, in the current debate about young people's fantasy and computer games, where there have been a number of comments and criticisms by Christians arguing that such products are harmful, a number of enthusiasts, arguing from a secular position, have come to the defence of the products. Very often their argument goes something like this: 'Here is a statement by somebody who says they are a Christian, attacking what I enjoy doing. I'm a Christian [here follows a definition of what they consider a Christian to be] and I don't think it's harmful. Therefore the criticism is invalid.'

The debate about fantasy is a complex one, and it has to be said that Christians have occasionally made some very ill-informed and unhelpful contributions to it. But the definitions which are given of Christianity by the 'other side' are often weak and inaccurate. For many, Christianity is considered to be merely a moral code, often separated from meaningful church involvement. For others it means subscribing to a set of fairly liberal values. For others it means not deliberately hurting other people. In several years of studying the debate, I have never heard anybody talking in it about Christianity as a commitment to a personal God, or even talking about Christianity as something that made strong demands on the individual claiming to be a Christian. Many of those who claimed to be Christians did not see it as much of a distinctive at all, and many who quoted the Bible were either inaccurate or chose particularly inappropriate passages to argue their case.

Politicians, too, frequently use the word 'Christianity' in a loose way to denote a bag of ethical and values which they generally endorse. The 'social gospel' has been very attractive to some (particularly socialist) political thinkers, who have seen in Jesus Christ a socialist activist and have admired much of the Bible. Here is George Bernard Shaw, for example, allowing some merit (mainly literary) to Scripture in the preface to a short story that has been regarded by many Christians as one of the most destructive attacks on biblical Christianity ever written – *The Black Girl in Search of God:*

> The fact remains that a great deal of the Bible is much more alive than this morning's paper and last night's parliamentary debate. Its chronicles are better reading than most of our fashionable histories, and less intentionally mendacious. In revolutionary invective and Utopian inspiration it cuts the ground from under the feet of Ruskin, Carlyle and Karl Marx; and in epics of great leaders and great rascals it makes Homer seem superficial and Shakespear unbalanced. And its one great love poem is the only one that can satisfy a man who is really in

> love. Shelley's Epipsychidion is, in comparison, literary gas and gaiters.[30]

Shaw's grudging praise comes in the middle of a scathing attack on the Bible, yet in his writings he often turned to the teaching of Jesus and occasionally to specific Bible passages to validate social concerns. Some socialists have gone much further, and argued that Christianity is the inspiration and source of socialism without which socialism would be immeasurably impoverished. Thus Donald Soper reflected, 'Christianity gave socialism its legs' (to which Malcolm Muggeridge mischievously replied, 'Ah yes, Donald! But look where those legs have carried it . . .').[31] Soper, of course, spoke as a Methodist minister, but Shaw was an iconoclast who rejected the core of Soper's belief. He was one of many who would accept much of the Sermon on the Mount while rejecting its author's view of his own identity.

Clearly, a politician who defended a course of action, policy or political programme by reference to such a partial or distorted view of Christianity should be corrected. Indeed, if a politician's entire political judgement was based on an erroneous view of Scripture or a misunderstanding of the Christian faith he or she would, once that misunderstanding had been pointed out authoritatively, be vulnerable to demands for resignation. And it is the task of Christians to correct such misunderstandings, which might at times bring them into political controversy. Where the politician has used Christian arguments while himself or herself rejecting Christianity for themselves, the controversy should be all the keener. If the church and state find themselves at loggerheads on this issue, it is an argument in which the church has every right to be involved.

30. Bernard Shaw, *The Black Girl in Search of God: and Some Lesser Tales* (1932: Penguin edn, n d), p 15.
31. Quoted by Malcolm Muggeridge in conversation with the author.

Mis-applying Christianity

A rather different situation is that when a politician clearly has some meaningful commitment to Christianity but does not translate that into a recognisably biblical concept of politics. Many politicians are Christians (in Britain, the House of Commons Christian fellowship groups have a respectable membership), and many more seem to have considerable understanding of what the core issues of Christianity really are (some of the political discussion over the ordination of women in 1993/4, for example, was noticeably well-informed). But the notion of 'Christian politics' belongs properly only to a political understanding that is shaped by biblical distinctives and would change significantly were the biblical elements removed. Not all Christian politicians, by this definition, are engaged in Christian politics, though they are probably doing their job with integrity and commitment.

American politics provides at least two examples of different styles of Christian presidency. President Ronald Reagan was known to be a church-goer. He did not seek to disguise his faith when running for President and he often spoke as a God-fearing man. But in office he seemed to make few connections between that faith and the governing of America. President Jimmy Carter, whose evangelical faith prompted much discussion (and some abuse) during the election campaign, seemed by contrast to be making a substantial effort to consider what difference his faith should make to how he did his job – a separate issue, of course, from that of the political qualities of the two men as presidents.

A striking British example was provided in 1988 when on 21 May Prime Minister Margaret Thatcher addressed the General Assembly of the Church of Scotland.[32] She introduced her speech by saying, 'Perhaps it would be best if I

32. The full text of her speech is included as an Appendix in: Michael Alison and David L Edwards (eds), *Christianity and Conservatism* (Hodder & Stoughton, 1990), p 333.

began by speaking personally as a Christian, as well as a politician, about the way I see things.'

I know nothing about Baroness Thatcher that would make me want to dispute her claim to be a Christian, and her overall three-point summary of Christian belief which she offered the Assembly contains no major omissions or deviations from biblical truth. Her quotation from 'When I survey the wondrous Cross,' too, gives the impression that she knows the hymn rather than that a researcher has found it for her (even though by this point the characteristically Thatcherian theme of taking responsibility for your own welfare – physical and spiritual – has begun to emerge).

Some problems begin to appear, however, when she goes on to describe how she sees her faith and her political activities relating:

> May I also say a few words about my personal belief in the relevance of Christianity to public policy – to the things that are Caesar's? The Old Testament lays down in Exodus the Ten Commandments as given to Moses, the injunction in Leviticus to love our neighbours as ourselves and generally the importance of observing a strict code of law. The New Testament is a record of the Incarnation, the teachings of Christ and the establishment of the Kingdom of God. Again we have the emphasis of loving our neighbour as ourselves and to 'Do-as-you-would-be-done-by'. I believe that by taking together these two elements from the Old and New Testaments we gain a view of the universe, a proper social attitude to work, and principles to shape economic and social life.

Lady Thatcher's first example of this was Paul, speaking to the Thessalonians: 'If a man will not work, he shall not eat' (2 Thess. 3:10). She quoted this to reinforce her assertion that 'We are told we must work and use our talents to create wealth.' But a reading of Paul's comments in context shows that he was making two points: firstly, that work is necessary to avoid the idler becoming dependent on others; and secondly, that those who do not work become busybodies. In other words, Paul's warning is intended to prevent undesirable consequences, not to create desirable ones. He is not talking about the generating of a wealth-economy, but about the proper functioning of able-bodied individuals within society.

From this exegesis Lady Thatcher argued that 'it is not the creation of wealth that is wrong but the love of money for its own sake', again making rather surprising use of the tenth Commandment to support her case and using a quotation from C S Lewis that not everybody will accept in this context.

Reactions to the speech were mixed. Some interpreted its strong defence of the value of the individual, responsibility for one's own welfare, wealth-creation and the emphasis on the two spheres of sovereignty of church and state, as the government's response to various criticisms of government policy by religious spokespeople (the Bishop of Durham had described those policies as 'wicked' in an Easter sermon only a few weeks previously). Others ridiculed the Prime Minister as ineptly attempting to teach the church theology.

But most accepted that it was, as Rachel Tingle described it, 'a moral and biblical defence of [Margaret Thatcher's] policies'.[33] She had said as much in the speech. She was attempting to use the Bible and the Christian gospel as justification for her government's actions.

By doing so she had launched a debate in which the church and the nation's Christians were involved by right. This was a subject in which they were expert. Those who felt that the Prime Minister had misunderstood and misapplied Scripture (and not everybody did think so) had every right to say so.

33. Rachel Tingle, *Another Gospel? An Account of the Growing Involvement of the Anglican Church in Secular Politics* (Christian Studies Centre, 1988), p 9.

Hypocrisy

The categories above often involve genuine misunderstanding, and many who misrepresent Christianity do so unintentionally and with respect. However, there have been occasions (some in recent years) when a politician has justified a social programme on the grounds that it is a moral programme intended to remedy abuses and to enforce moral behaviour. If that politician is then found to be guilty of the same moral lapses his programme is intended to control, then there is obviously a good case for his resignation; and certainly every reason, for those who think that morality and integrity are important, to publicly critique the politician in question.

The moral maze

But is that as far as it goes? Is the only situation where Christians are allowed to criticise politics that in which Christianity has been distorted or misunderstood, or where there has been clear moral failure? If so, the Christian voice is doomed to remain marginalised, becoming relevant only when the precise nature of the margin needs defining.

But Christianity has a bigger stake.

Like politics, Christian action is the working out of a world view in practice. It has values it wishes to promote, proposals of its own, an agenda for change, and a vision of how people ought to behave in a fair and just society.

Contrary to what many people believe, so has politics:

> Every political decision, no matter how complex or in what area, is always informed by certain ideas. Politicians always justify their decisions; they regard such and such a measure desirable because it is just; because it promotes liberty; because it serves the common good; because it is demanded by public interest. But what liberty really is, or justice, or welfare is decided by every politician as it were, for himself. Such deciding is loosely connected with his

> total view of life. All such concepts as liberty, justice etc. are only clearing houses for the deep convictions of each politician. Whether he wants to or not, his own perspective on life will break through into the world of practical politics because of the content which he gives to these ideas and concepts. (*Bob Goudzwaard*)[34]

Therefore Christians *can* take a great deal of interest in politics, and *should* do so, if only in order to scrutinise what agendas and values are being offered and to determine, where they coincide with those of Christianity, whether they are acceptable. Politics is a public debate that extends far beyond the formal chambers of the House of Commons and the House of Lords. It is a debate that is carried on – with greater and lesser success – in the media, in the workplace, wherever people meet. The church as part of that community has an obligation to become involved in the discussion.

We have already seen that much of the political task is independent of the church and that it would be wrong to demand that the church be given any right of involvement in that area. The point at which the church can and should begin to engage in dialogue with the politicians is that in which the state begins to talk the language of morality.

The basis for action

Moral arguments are often used to justify political decisions, as Goudzwaard explains above. The Chancellor of the Exchequer will argue that a particular tax should be increased, because it will generate the cash to pay needed benefits or will subsidise tax cuts in other parts of the economy. An industry spokesman will recommend closing a factory with the loss of jobs, on the grounds that it will lead to a leaner, stronger economy which will eventually generate

34. Bob Goudzwaard, *A Christian Political Option* (Wedge, Canada, 1972), p 31.

far more jobs than the ones that were lost. Admission charges to art galleries might be justified on the grounds that what is essentially a minority interest should be funded at least in part by the people who benefit from it most, and defence cuts are frequently justified with the argument that the world has changed, that old enmities have died, and fewer weapons and forces are now needed.

Many of such grounds for action are technical matters, requiring expert knowledge. There is nothing in the Bible that equips the Christian church as an organisation to be expert at industrial forecasts, economic analysis or management of the labour force. Of course individual Christians will be gifted and trained in such matters, will (hopefully) bring a particular Christian perspective to them, and may even in some cases make politics their career. But their primary qualification for speaking on these matters will be that they know something about them, not that they are Christians.

So where *does* Christianity have a voice?

A moral mandate

The Church must clearly become involved when politicians appeal to morality as the basis for their policies.

When politicians claim that a particular course of action or decision is not merely pragmatic, nor that it is merely advantageous to the overall economy, nor that it is merely appropriate to a changed situation, but that it is *morally the proper course of action*, then Christians must examine the matter, for this is an area in which the church *does* possess expertise.

Cynics have often portrayed politicians as pragmatic, hard-boiled people who tend to do things out of expediency and self-interest. There may well be a higher proportion of such people in politics than in other occupations, because politics offers the promise of power and influence. But the most casual listening to politicians shows that the majority are driven by a sense of commitment to a set of ideals and a desire to serve. Whether it be somebody like Tony Benn, teaching Labour ideology to small groups in draughty village halls far from Westminster, or the 'Gang of Four' leaving their party for the political wilderness, or a Government spokesperson defending an unpopular policy on television's *Question Time*, the spectacle of a politician holding to a matter of moral principle at some personal cost is by no means uncommon. 'These were not easy decisions for me to take,' wrote Jimmy Carter, recalling the Panama Canal issue:

> I knew that we were sure to face a terrible political fight in Congress. . . . Furthermore, public opinion polls showed that the American public strongly opposed relinquishing control of the canal. . . . Nevertheless, I believed that a new treaty was absolutely necessary. I was convinced that we needed to correct an injustice.[35]

For Carter it was both a political issue and a moral one, but his moral judgement informed his political arguments, as when he describes those of his opponents:

> Governor Ronald Reagan gave the Panama Canal issue special prominence during the 1976 presidential primaries. . . . He repeatedly used a line guaranteed to get applause: 'When it comes to the Canal, we built it, we paid for it, it's ours and we should tell Torrijos and Company that we are going to keep it!' Reagan's position appealed to many Americans, because he presented the issue, simplistically, as a test of our nation's power and greatness.[36]

Jimmy Carter was not the only politician to have taken deeply unpopular decisions out of moral conviction, but few political autobiographies have such unsparing honesty as his

35. Jimmy Carter, *Keeping Faith: Memoirs of a President* (Collins, 1982), p 155.
36. Ibid, p 154.

Keeping Faith (1982). In it, he reveals an attitude to politics that is often expressed as moral choices.

The moral umbrella

This might seem to be leading us to a simple and easily-understood conclusion that could be summed up like this: Christianity and politics are two separate spheres, not mutually exclusive but interacting where one strays into the territory of the other. Thus Christians, as Christians, have no right of comment when government pronounces on the price of grapefruit; but when government attempts to define Christianity or make moral judgements, Christians can and must get involved.

It's a tempting conclusion, but it rests on a misunderstanding. The implication is that human experience can be portrayed like this:

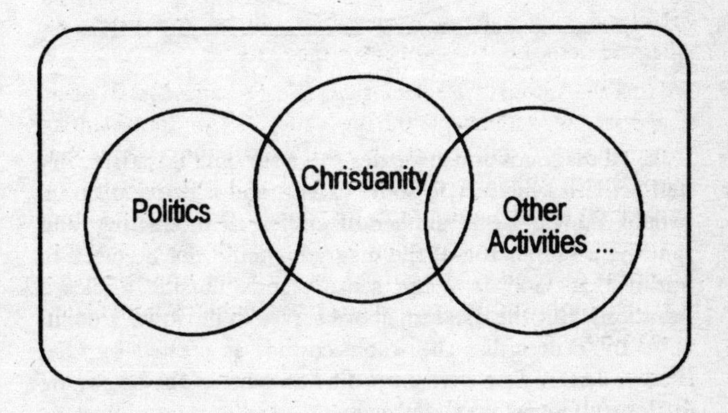

But the biblical model is quite different, and can be represented like this:

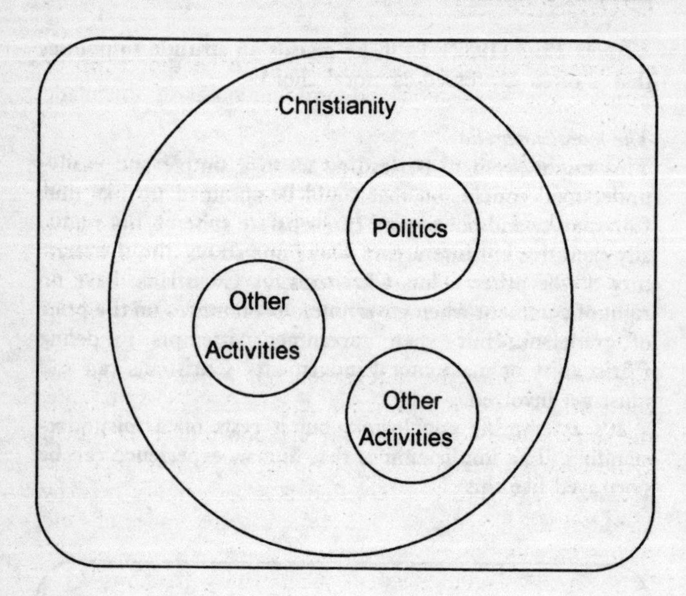

Like all diagrams and analogies these are both unsatisfactory (all activities interact to some extent, and a better diagram would show a large number of circles all interacting; and putting a border round the diagram should not be taken to mean that God in some sense stands outside a closed creation). But the diagram above serves to illustrate a point. The Bible describes the whole cosmos as created by God and under God's sovereignty. The account at the beginning of John's Gospel is all-embracing:

> In the beginning was the Word, and the Word was with God, and the Word was God. He was with God in the beginning. Through him all things were made; without him nothing was made that has been made (John 1:1–3).

When the process of that creation is described in the book

of Genesis, human beings are shown to be the crown of creation, the integration and ordering point of the made world:

> Then God said, 'Let us make man in our image, in our likeness, and let them rule over the fish of the sea and the birds of the air, over the livestock, over all the earth, and over all the creatures that move along the ground.' So God created man in his own image, in the image of God he created him; male and female he created them (Genesis 1:26–27).

The story of how that integration was broken by the fall and restored by the incarnation and crucifixion of Jesus is the story of the gospel. But the creation model set out in Genesis and restored in Christ is that the sovereignty that human beings hold over creation is a sovereignty held by virtue of the fact that we are created in the image of God who is holy and morally perfect.

So in the second diagram, Christianity is shown as a circle embracing all other circles. Biblical morality cannot be separated from the Christian gospel and the moral character of God. It is like an umbrella, bringing together under it the entire created world. No human activity lies outside the sphere of morality, for no human activity lies outside the ambit of the sovereignty of God who is absolute morality.

Thus argues the Bible, and we shall be looking at further biblical texts in Chapter Five.

The consequences for Christians engaging with politics are not hard to work out. In the biblical perspective all decisions involve moral choices, all policies are moral or immoral, all government acts and programmes can be measured by the yardstick of whether or not they are right or wrong. Christian involvement is not limited to providing expert input when politicians attempt to define what Christianity is. Nor is it limited to making an informed contribution when politicians appeal to morality and religion as justification for their actions and policies. All political decisions are moral decisions. All politics is ultimately a debate about what is moral or desirable and in that debate Christians have a stake and a voice.

The situation was well summed up by William Temple in his influential *Christianity and Social Order* (1942):

> If a bridge is to be built, the Church may remind the engineer that it is his obligation to provide a really safe bridge; but it is not entitled to tell him whether, in fact, his design meets this requirement; a particular theologian may also be a competent engineer, and, if he is, his judgement on this point is entitled to attention; but this is altogether because he is a competent engineer and his theological equipment has nothing whatever to do with it. In just the same way the Church may tell the politician what ends the social order should promote; but it must leave to the politician the devising of the precise means to those ends.[37]

To which it might be added that individual Christians, as citizens, are entitled to express an opinion about the 'means' as well, both in discussion and by the ballot box; and in this their Christian faith must also be relevant.

37. William Temple, *Christianity and Social Order* (Penguin, 1942), p 35. Temple is mentioned further in Chapter Four.

3

'WHAT ONE HOLDS DEAR': A SELECTION OF VIEWS

When we want to understand the moral perspectives of a previous age, one helpful resource is the novels of the period. In the descriptions of characters and the author's own reflections, values and moral priorities usually emerge clearly, irrespective of the literary quality of the work.

I want in this chapter to use fiction as such a guide. If 'back to basics' is a good direction to go, what are the 'basics' to which we must return? We will look at some of the values that have been suggested or implied by various writers as being those that endure; values which are necessary if a society is to be admirable, and which we lose at our peril; and from where those values are derived.

Secular basics

As we saw at the beginning of this book, most quests for values tend to look backwards rather than forward, for those who look for them are usually disillusioned with the present and pessimistic about the future. Many visions of an alternative future are rural, such as that described by William Morris, whose picture of the future is optimistic but is drawn from an idyllic pastoral golden age.

The basics of Nowhere

Morris's hero in *News From Nowhere* (1890) has woken up to find himself in a London of the distant future, a 'fully-developed new society'. He readily finds guides who are very willing to talk to this visitor from the past:

> I looked to the right again, and said, in a rather doubtful tone of voice, 'Why! There are the Houses of Parliament! Do you still use them?'
>
> He burst out laughing, and was some time before he could control himself; then he clapped me on the back and said:
>
> 'I take you, neighbour; you may well wonder at our keeping them standing, and I know something about that, and my old kinsman has given me books to read about the strange game that they played there. Use them! Well, yes, they are used for a sort of subsidiary market, and a storage place for manure, and they are handy for that, being on the water-side. . . . You know at the worst these silly old buildings serve as a kind of foil to the beautiful ones which we build now. You will see several others in these parts; the place my great grandfather lives in, for instance, and a big building called St. Paul's. And you see, in this matter we need not grudge a few poorish buildings standing, because we can always build elsewhere . . .'[38]

It is interesting that rural visions of the future are almost always utopian, and technological ones are almost always nightmares. . . . It must be said that even in Morris's time his vision of a pastoral future cannot have been much consolation to those who lived in the teeming streets of Victorian London, who must have been as depressed by the remoteness of the vision as by the scale of civil strife that was necessary to bring it into being. But it is an attractive picture he paints;

38. William Morris, *News From Nowhere: Being Some Chapters From a Utopian Romance* (1890), ch 5.

that of a society stripped of extraneous and selfish values, a society that has truly gone back to basics.

Those basics for Morris primarily reflected his own emphasis on craftsmanship. It is striking how contemporary Morris's values for the arts are. They are certainly echoed by opinions such as those of Paul Johnson in a March 1994 television discussion about whether there should be a cultural 'back to basics';[39] he argued, like Morris, that buildings should be designed with the consent of those who had to live in them, and that there was a lamentable absence of skill in much admired contemporary art. Thus for Morris, the excesses of Victorian art and architecture were to be rejected in favour of design that married utility and beauty.

In economics, Morris prophesied his ideal society as one that has outgrown currency and conducted itself on the basis of mutual concern and the spontaneous and unselfish filling of other people's needs, a system that has replaced 'extinct commercial morality'. Personal property is no longer a meaningful word. Idleness is no longer a problem, for everybody enjoys their work. Slums are a thing of the past, for people who want space live in houses in the meadows, and the city centres are full of gregarious people who prefer to live close to others out of choice. Industry has long gone, the factories have been pulled down, and the labouring communities dispersed. International tension no longer exists, and as for politics – 'We have none.'

Reading *News From Nowhere*, it is easy to identify what the basics were for Morris, because his hero has them spelt out to him at every opportunity. They derive from the socialist ideal of the perfectibility of human beings. The message that runs through the book is that were one to remove the difficulties and burdens that shackle people, then everybody would be happy and everybody would be good. In Morris's utopia, grief and wickedness are abnormalities.

Central among Morris's basic values is the dignity and

39. *The Late Show*, BBC2, 15 March 1994.

worth of human beings. Freed from an unrepresentative, oppressive government and unfair law courts, people are now happy. This spiritual regeneration has not come about through religion, which has been long since discarded, but through freedom from oppression. Now what establishes individual worth is the dignity of labour. Art has taken the place of commercial competition, and is now an accepted element of production; and the imagination is encouraged by folk art and storytelling.

Morris (who contributed immensely to the Arts and Craft movement) defined art as 'the expression of man's delight in his labour', and the love of labour is basic to his utopia. Children grow up and enter work because they have seen their elders working and want to do the same. Basic, too, is the love of knowledge for its own sake. Literacy is only the beginning – modern languages and Greek and Latin are commonly studied. Thus in Morris's arts-oriented, pastoral, technologically indifferent utopia (drawing heavily on a somewhat idealised version of the Middle Ages), the values that are central are those that emphasise the individuality, worth, creativity and essential generosity of human beings. The message of his book is that what Victorian society needed most of all was to strip away greed, ambition, the dehumanising toil of slavery and human bitterness of every kind, and get back to basic people values. Man is born free, he might have said, and is everywhere in chains . . .

Values of social order

Morris was a founding father of British socialism; John Buchan came from the other end of the political spectrum, a product of the Scottish upper classes, a child of the manse who went on to senior diplomatic office.

Morris's dream of the future looked back to the past of the Middle Ages chiefly because that was a period with art that appealed to him and a tradition of dignified artisanship – a dream that he attempted to make into a partial reality in his home at Kelmscott, his printing press and his work with the Pre-Raphaelite Brotherhood.

Buchan in his books looked back to a different, more recent past. Like Morris he was a man of some means (classically educated, he pursued careers in journalism and law before, as Lord Tweedsmuir, becoming governor-general of Canada), but was less embarrassed by it. He could be described as a belated product of the same Victorian society that Morris rejected.

Of his many books the best-known are the Richard Hannay adventures, the exploits of a wealthy South African mining engineer who became a British major and hunted spies – his career reflects Buchan's own service in South Africa after the Boer War. No doubt because he was a member of a privileged class under threat from social change and war – he wrote the first Hannay books during the First World War, and died in 1940 – Buchan's books often contain elegies for a vanishing way of life and for values that seem perilously close to extinction.

> She belonged to the out-of-doors and to the old house and to the world at large. She belonged to the war, and to that happier world beyond it – a world which must be won by going through the struggle and not by shirking it.[40]

> We stopped to look out of the long staircase window which showed a segment of lawn, a corner of the lake, and through a gap in the woods a vista of green downland. Mary squeezed my arm. 'What a blessed country,' she said. 'Dick, did you ever dream of such peace? We're lucky, lucky people.'
>
> Then suddenly her face changed. . . . 'It's too good and beloved to last,' she whispered. 'Sometimes I am afraid.'[41]

For Buchan, the basic values are those of the British country

40. John Buchan, *Mr Standfast* (1918), ch 1.
41. John Buchan, *The Three Hostages* (1924), ch 1.

gentleman, and are often symbolised by land, whether it be the peaceful South African veldt or the tranquil Scottish countryside. Qualities such as loyalty, integrity, law-keeping and service to one's country have an almost religious force in his novels, and the overthrow of such values is tantamount to the dawn of a new dark age:

> He began by saying,. . . . A large part of the world had gone mad, and that involved the growth of inexplicable and unpredictable crime. All the old sanctities had become weakened, and men had grown too well accustomed to death and pain. This meant that the criminal had far greater resources at his command, and, if he were an able person, could mobilize a vast amount of utter recklessness and depraved ingenuity. The moral imbecile, he said, had been more or less a sport [= *freak*] before the War: now he was a terribly common product, and throve in batches and battalions. Cruel, humourless, hard, utterly wanting in sense of proportion, but often full of a perverted poetry and drunk with rhetoric – a hideous, untameable breed had been engendered. You found it among the young Bolshevik Jews, among the young entry of the wilder Communist sects, and very notably among the sullen murderous hobbledehoys in Ireland.
>
> 'Poor devils,' Macgillivray repeated. 'It is for their Maker to judge them, but we who are trying to patch up civilization have to see that they are cleared out of the world.'[42]

It is noticeable in Buchan's novels that the possession of these values depends either on having the wealth to enjoy them or on being part of a classless cameraderie of free men, wandering at will through the world defending the old ways.

Buchan's values acquire added poignancy from the threat of extinction in the face of war; there is a similar poignancy

42. Ibid, ch 2.

in Siegfried Sassoon and in Rupert Brooke's longing for England –

> Her sights and sounds; dreams happy as her day;
> And laughter, learnt of friends; and gentleness,
> In hearts at peace, under an English heaven.[43]

But there is a very similar note in certain peace-time novels. A typical quotation (intriguing because it encapsulates so many of its author's prejudices) is this from Dornford Yates:

> Daphne Pleydell would have distinguished any age. A famous beauty, she steadfastly refused to allow any picture of herself to appear in the public prints. As the hostess of White Ladies, as of her London home, she displayed an efficiency, dignity and charm seldom encountered severally, never together. Her servants worshipped her; men, old and young, were proud to sit at her feet; all women bore her goodwill. She was all things to one man – her husband. Gentle in fair weather, gallant in foul; gay, resolute; honest, wise and kind, she was for all time a model of excellence.[44]

The values of Yates, Buchan and many like them are the values of social stability, a hierarchy that works from the point of view of the person celebrating it. While servants and labourers are often spoken of with respect and affection, they are static elements of the hierarchy moving neither up nor down the social ladder, and often their function is to reinforce the established order (in Yates a servant who has served for many years, or has been one of the character's batmen in the war, is rewarded with an exceptionally appreciative employer). We do not hear the employee's point of view, which might turn out to be quite different, for what seems to be a harmonious whole might turn out to be resting on exploitation and drudgery.

43. Rupert Brooke, 'The Soldier', *1914 and Other Poems* (1915).
44. Dornford Yates, *The House that Berry Built* (Ward Lock, 1945), p 185.

The characters who dominate the novels of Buchan and those like him would list among the basic values those of service and loyalty, and would see their own service and loyalty to their country as a parallel to the service they enjoyed from their servants. The War, of course, threatens this relationship in many ways. After the war those leisured days will be gone never to return. The rolling gentle landscape of the Scottish estate may well be split up to pay death duties, or the death of heirs might change everything. The gillies and manservants who looked after the landed families may well find themselves newly employable elsewhere, and their wives who worked in the munitions factories, on the land and in service industries will no longer be as ready to wait at table and light coal fires.

In this perspective, basic values become those values which are considered central to a social order to which not everybody belongs. They are values because they create a world of aspirations and achievements, and they are basic because without them the order would collapse.

Versions of truth

I have quoted two ends of a spectrum, and both contain elements of truth. As a Christian I sympathise with William Morris's emphasis on the dignity of the individual and his insistence that work should be joy rather than a burden. As somebody earning his living in the making of books I warm to his thoughts about the value of art. But biblically, there is a flaw in his argument that is fatal, for it is a misunderstanding of something that is central to his case.

Morris believed in the perfectibility of human beings. He believed that the only thing that stopped men and women being good, honest, caring and compassionate was the burdens laid upon them by the people who exploited them. Take away the ugliness of modern life, he argued, the grinding economic treadmill and the greed of those who controlled industry, and people would be happy. In his England of the future there was no government, because people would no longer commit crime. There was no property, because nobody would be selfish or greedy. There were no wars and no urban problems, because human beings would live peaceably together.

History demonstrates the opposite. The story of the human race bears out the biblical argument that there is something that makes us tend to do what is wrong in preference to what is right, to prefer ugliness to beauty and anger to love. Yet there is ample evidence too that humanity bears the imprint of God's image, that art and craft are areas in which men and women can create beauty, that we have the capability of running against the bias of our flawed humanity.

Morris's utopia is not nonsense. Creativity, contentedness and kindness are neither meaningless nor impossible ideals. He had identified genuine 'basic' values, rooted in the value and worth of the individual. His mistake was in believing that all that stood between his society and that of his book was the exploitative society in which he lived; that if left alone, mankind could gain happiness on its own. Morris recognised the basics, but proposed an inadequate way back to them.

John Buchan might appear at first to be much less justifiable biblically; Dornford Yates even less so. But the Victorian values they admired did contain much that was characteristically Christian, though often scarcely presented as such.

Take for example Buchan's Macgillivray, castigating the new wartime criminals. On one level he is a kind of right-wing blimp demonstrating attitudes and prejudices commonly identified as 'right-wing'; you can hear very similar speeches at most Conservative Party conferences, with some extremely draconian punishment programmes being proposed from the conference floor (occasionally, as in the 'short sharp shock' proposals, echoed from the platform).

Yet somewhere in Macgillivray's rhetoric is an echo of the Bible's emphasis on justice and the punishment of the wrongdoer. He had little sympathy (at least in the speech I have quoted) for any notion of rehabilitative justice, and he talked in terms of eradicating, rather than reclaiming, the sinner; no prodigal son here. But there is no doubt that the punishment of crime is a basic Christian value.

It is a Christian value not because it satisfies society's desire for vengeance, nor even because it ensures that the community is protected from unrestrained criminals. The Christian value of punishment was well explained by C S Lewis in an essay critiquing a secular theory:

> According to the Humanitarian theory, to punish a man because he deserves it, and as much as he deserves, is mere revenge, and therefore, barbarous and immoral. . . . My contention is that this doctrine, merciful though it appears, really means that each one of us, from the moment he breaks the law, is deprived of the rights of a human being.
>
> The reason is this. The Humanitarian theory removes from Punishment the concept of Desert. But the concept of Desert is the only connecting link between punishment and justice. It is only as deserved or undeserved that a sentence can be just or unjust. . . . The Humanitarian theory wants simply to abolish Justice and substitute Mercy for it. This means you start being 'kind' to people before you have considered their rights, and then force upon them supposed kindnesses which no one but you will recognise as kindnesses and which the recipient will recognise as abominable cruelties. You have overshot the mark. Mercy, detached from Justice, grows unmerciful.[45]

Thus the rhetoric of Macgillivray, like Morris's dream, derives, in the long run, from the dignity and worth of the individual.

Buchan's frequent emphasis on land, despite being rooted in ownership and privilege – even if the just reward for

45. C S Lewis, 'The Humanitarian Theory of Punishment' in: Walter Hooper (ed), *C S Lewis: God in the Dock, Essays on Theology and Ethics* (Eerdmans, 1970), pp 287–8, 294.

years of faithful service to one's nation[46] – also has some biblical resonances. The Bible's discussion of land is a complex theological concept, but the relationship of people to it is crucial. Father Robert Farrar Capon points out the twentieth-century heresy:

> For place we substitute *space*. Think of the creek with its bank of reeds. It is a place. If it is to be saved, to be lifted up, to be kept as a part of the real history of this village, it must be saved for what it is, *for itself.* But that is hardly the most likely thing that will happen to it. The overwhelming temptation of the planners will be to bury it in a conduit and to plant macadam on its grave. And why? Because they will never have looked at it as a *place.* For them it will have been only an abstraction, something contained within co-ordinates on a civil engineer's map – a nice empty space which, once its natural intractabilities have been tamed, can be converted into their favorite kind of packaged *locale.*[47]

One further example from Buchan: patriotism as such is not a Christian virtue, and there are overtones that are distasteful to modern readers in Buchan's celebration of the British Empire (though it is misleading to judge him entirely from his fiction; his 1915–19, 24-volume *Nelson's History of the War*, some of which was written from the trenches, has been admired as being free from jingoism). Yet the novels often contain the theme that the 'Christian State' (the Empire) stands for certain values with which biblical Christians will immediately identify. For example, Buchan's often paternal-

46. This is as good a place as any to record my suspicion that the classically-educated Buchan drew some of Hannay's Scottish contentment from Virgil's *Georgics*, and to mention George Gissing's *The Private Papers of Henry Ryecroft* (1912) as a modern equivalent, in this context, to Virgil's celebration of retirement.
47. Robert Farrar Capon, *An Offering of Uncles: the Priesthood of Adam and the Shape of the World* (Harper & Row, 1967), p 17.

ist attitude to the colonies does sometimes reflect a concern for the rights of indigenous people, and he often displays a moral anger when he sees a weak nation threatened by an exploitative neighbour. There are echoes of an Old Testament concern for aliens and the oppressed in Buchan, and a crusading hatred of evil.

Buchan's 'theological' novel, *Witch Wood* (1927) is an exploration of Scottish antinomianism after the style of James Hogg; it finds a comparable excitement to that of a spy thriller in its tale of a coven composed of ordained ministers, so sure of their Calvinistic election that they engage in the black arts ('I took the Wud wi' ithers, but I kenned I was a redeemed soul and that the Lord wouldna cast me away . . .'). He has some good stories of pagan practice, too, that recall M R James; in them, paganism is satisfactorily denounced.[48]

But this does not make John Buchan a 'Christian novelist', and though biblical values can be found among those he celebrates this only proves the point; that most people have a sense of abiding values, but that some of those values are tied in to the need to establish and confirm the social, moral and political system in which they feel most secure; that among everybody's values, whether they be governor-general or a gentleman artisan, are some that derive from the Bible and can be regarded as absolutes.

Christian values?

It would be unfair to leave the matter judged by extremes, or indeed not to include a writer who is confessedly Christian. It might seem that we are spoilt for choice, for the Christian market has seen many novels that have taken values as their dominant theme.

48. Eg 'The Wind in the Portico' in: John Buchan, *The Runagates Club* (nd).

The Baker Street Mysteries

An example is the series of detective novels by Thomas Brace Haughey, featuring a character, Geoffrey Weston, a 'consulting detective' who lives in 31 Baker Street, London. Modelling himself on Sherlock Holmes and aided by his chronicler and assistant John Taylor, Weston is the only detective 'who – as Jimmy Carter would put it – has been born again'.

The novels, which are conventional thrillers in which the villains perpetrate crimes against morality and ethics, give Weston many opportunities to preach. Here he is, for example, expanding upon the subject of utopias which we have already discussed:

> 'I know you'll claim that when utopia is reached governments will wither away. But that's more mere speculation. You intimate religion is an instrument of bourgeoisie greed. But the only truly unselfish people I know, sir, are Christians – yes, even Christian preachers.'[49]

He provides ample bibliographical references for his withering denunciations of his victims: here he is confronting a liberal clergyman.

> I could see that Geoff was disturbed by the preacher's smug attitude. But he kept hold of his feelings. His voice, when he spoke, was soft and reasonable.
>
> 'Schweitzer, sir, never found the real historical Jesus because he began with the wrong presuppositions. And neither, I'm afraid, have you. You label me insane for believing that God isn't a bumbler. But let me point to a certain archbishop of Canterbury who holds my view. And I could name fifty modern theologians that echo my sentiments. Do you label such men as Packer, Schaeffer, Montgomery (and I could go on and on) as lunatics?

49. Thomas Brace Haughey, *The Case of the Maltese Treasure* (Bethany, 1979), p 107.

> Somehow they can read Jesus's statements about the kingdom and see inspiring truth – not error.'[50]

There are probably many Christians who rejoice to see such explicit discussion of Christianity in a book that, though published by a Christian publisher, is intended to be read by those who are not Christians. Admittedly not very well written, with wooden characterisation and some weak research (Haughey seems to think that the houses in Baker Street have gardens), such books nevertheless communicate their authors' understanding of Christian truth clearly.

The problem is that such books do not so much communicate values as issue a call to subscribe to a particular agenda. Of course many novelists write within a framework of biblical values; C S Lewis and J R R Tolkien do, and so do Graham Greene, Morris West and many others. But in such novelists the values are generated by a coherent world view intrinsic to the novel, whereas for Thomas Haughey the biblical values appear to be bolted on as an extra; they do not emerge from the narrative but are the hook on which the narrative hangs. There is therefore no sense of an appeal to return to basic values that were once commonly accepted, but rather an invitation to convert to a particular brand of the Christian faith. In fact, reading Haughey, one wonders whether he would accept any values other than those specifically inculcated by Christianity as 'basic' at all; for him the challenge seems not so much to return, but to turn.

We began by examining two novelists, both of whom looked back to a past that contained values they cherished; one speculating on a future in which those values would reign unchallenged, the other prepared to go to war to defend his values. I have suggested that in both cases, the concept of a set of basic values is shaped by other references, in William Morris's case by his belief in the perfectibility of humanity,

50. Ibid, p 65.

in John Buchan's case by his implication in the system of class and ownership that secured the values he loved. In the single example of a Christian author I quoted (an extreme case but unfortunately not a rare one), we find again that there is no real appeal to some theoretical package of 'basic values', but instead a challenge to accept a systematic apologetic.

At the heart of the discussion, and to varying degrees at the heart of the books I have quoted, is the question: is there some set of values which are basic to a good and just society, to which all reasonable men and women of goodwill ought to assent because they are demonstrably valuable? Is there some moral package that can be defined as worthy of public acceptance in the same way that Bishop Lesslie Newbigin has defined Public Truth – as 'that which all men ought to accept as truth because it is true'?[51]

It may be that the concept of 'basics' is itself a weak idea, if it means some discoverable common moral ground to which we can call society back. Certain values are held to be excellent by all who subscribe to the dignity of human beings and the belief that it is better to do good than evil. Christianity argues that such values are derived from the Christian faith and are ultimately expressions of the holiness of God; that it is the activity of the Holy Spirit in the world that makes such values respected. A certain number of those values can be legislated, and they are summarised in the Ten Commandments; some have entered our cultural heritage and are summarised by the 'seven cardinal virtues'.

Because of what theologians have termed Common Grace – the grace of God shown to all human beings by virtue of their being made in his likeness and living in the world he created and described as good – it is not necessary to be a Christian to appreciate these values. Some who are not Christians have appreciated them more than some who are.

51. Said by Bishop Newbigin in open discussion at the July 1992 *Gospel And Our Culture* consultation.

When people talk of Plato as a Christian before Christ, they refer to his ethical understanding and moral integrity in so far as these are in accordance with biblical teaching. In the same way, for many people John Buchan is a 'Christian gentleman' and William Morris an early exponent of the 'Social Gospel'.

That is why some authors who are not Christians reach very close to the heart of Christian values. Here is Terry Pratchett, describing two witches ruminating at the end of an adventure:

> Magrat looked down at the brown river and the suspicious logs on its sand banks.
> 'What I want to know is,' she said, 'was Mrs Gogol really good or bad? I mean, dead people and alligators and everything . . .'
> Granny looked at the rising sun, poking through the mists.
> 'Good and bad is tricky,' she said. 'I ain't too certain about where people stand. P'raps what matters is which way you face.'[52]

Nevertheless Pratchett's refusal to be dogmatic and his compassion towards the frailties of his creations actually broadens out the theological discussion at the point where many Christians would want to narrow it and constrain it to a denominational or other formula. There is nothing wrong with formulas, and the Bible makes it clear that there are certain indispensable requirements without which nobody will be saved. But these are not denominational requirements, but relational ones, to do with 'which way one faces'. You cannot achieve salvation by an unfocused compassion or a vague sense of the desirability of virtue. That tends to lead to relativism, and it is because the Bible speaks concretely about morals that so many Christians hate relativism. As Elaine Storkey observes,

52. Terry Pratchett, *Witches Abroad* (Corgi, 1991), p 285.

> What has been so unsettling is the feeling that we need a single moral standard on most of the fundamental issues of life: where it is as wrong to lie as to mug: as wrong to embezzle as it is to commit arson. In our days of relativist morality the rallying cry of universal and abiding morals is a deeply attractive one. . . . Yet it has never been clear for me where going back to our basic morals would have taken us anyway. There is a question whether society has ever observed an impartial, universal set of standards which contains no bias, and favours no group. What is closer to the truth is that there has always been a tendency for people to construct a morality which suits them.[53]

Perhaps the message of the authors we have considered is that 'back to basics' in each case would mean returning to a basic morality that they themselves defined and which was acceptable to, and by implication favoured, them.

This is hardly Christian morality, whatever the size of the lobby supporting it.

53. Elaine Storkey, *Thought for the Day*, BBC Radio 4, 12 January 1994.

4

MORAL GOVERNMENT: A SELECTION OF VIEWS

From the question of values we turn in this chapter to the other question that concerns us in this book. To what extent is it appropriate to require that those who govern us should be morally accountable? Which is more important; that the law be moral, or that law-makers and political leaders should be moral? We shall look at these themes in the work of a number of writers.

For some these issues have seemed very straightforward, and to none have they appeared so uncomplicated as to those contemplating an ideal society. So let us begin with two such writers who are separated by centuries: Plato and T S Eliot.

The Republic and its Laws: Plato

> There have been plenty of good statesmen here in Athens and have been as good in the past. The question is, have they also been good teachers of their own virtue?[54]

The philosopher Plato (c 429–347 BC) devoted much space in his Socratic dialogues to the notion that one could teach virtue, just as one could teach mathematics or grammar. It

54. Plato, *The Meno*, para 93.

was held that it was possible to be educated into moral behaviour. It is an issue he addressed in *The Meno*, in which Meno asks Socrates forthrightly, 'Can you tell me . . . is virtue something that can be taught? Or does it come by practice? Or is it neither teaching nor practice that gives it to a man but natural aptitude or something else?[55]

Meno received only a partial answer, the discussion foundering on the vexed question of whether virtue was the same thing as knowledge: but in *The Republic* Plato returned to the theme at length.

> For Plato the object of education is exclusively moral. Literature and music are studied not for their own sake but in order that through them the young may become good citizens and good men, temperate, brave, wise and just. Moreover, every element in our environment affects our character for good or evil. . . . Who will rule in this city? The answer comes easily: those of the guardians who show the greatest concern for its welfare. . . . Book III ends with an outline of the life which rulers and auxiliaries are to lead. They will have no private property and live in barracks in austere, disciplined austerity.[56]

Thus R M Hare summarises the beginning of what is to be a lengthy discourse, parts of which are impractical and a few of which are sometimes distasteful to modern ears (and possibly to Plato's contemporaries) – for example, the ideal republic would breed its rulers to order on 'stud farms', and cull any unworthy offspring ruthlessly. Obviously the main argument is subtle and complex, but an essential strand of Plato's thinking is clear to see. Virtue *can* and *should* be taught; and if that is the case, then we ought to be looking

55. Plato, trs W K C Guthrie, *Protagoras* and *Meno* (Penguin 1956), p 115.
56. Plato, trs Benjamin Jowett, ed. R M Hare and D A Russell, *The Republic* (Sphere Books, 1970), Hare's introduction to Bk III, p 45.

closely at the people who are doing the teaching. In other words, if there are those who adopt the role of teaching the community how to live virtuous lives, then the moral quality of their own lives must come under scrutiny.

Plato was constructing his argument in terms of an ideal republic, and he inevitably concluded that its rulers would have to be philosophers. His later dialogue *The Laws* is usually regarded as *The Republic* made practical, an examination of how the ideal principles of *The Republic* might be worked out in a world that had to settle for less then the ideal. In the earlier dialogue the ideal ruler is one who is an expert in the moral law; in the later work his place is largely taken by the detailed moral code of law itself which governs the life of the community. At the back of the law is religion, to which all citizens must subscribe. The highest instruments of government are the Guardians of the Laws.

Significantly, in this 'real-world' discussion Plato once again emphasises the moral accountability of the Guardians. As Trevor Saunders summarises,

> The Guardians, whose tenure and powers make them tolerably independent of popular pressures, should themselves obey the laws in all things, and interpret them when necessary in the spirit in which they were framed. Yet even they are not exempt from the general rule that every official must be accountable for his conduct. . . . One authority must check another; firm government must not be allowed to degenerate into tyranny.[57]

There appears to be a sense in Plato that the ultimate accountability of governors and guardians is religion. Consequently it does not matter whether virtue (described in *The Meno* as being almost like a poet's inspiration) can or cannot be systematically taught; for the rulers point to the same source of virtue, to which they ought to lead the people.

57. Plato, trs Trevor J Saunders, *The Laws* (Penguin, 1970), Saunders's introduction, p 33.

The Idea of a Christian Society: T S Eliot

T S Eliot (1888–1965) published the long essay *The Idea of a Christian Society* in October 1939. It was based on three Cambridge lectures, delivered the previous June. He was already known for his early poems (*Prufrock*, 1917, and *The Waste Land*, 1922, for example), and for his Christian poetry (*Ash Wednesday*, 1930 and the early poems from *Four Quartets*). He had published his first play in 1932, and had established his reputation as a critic with such collections of essays as *The Sacred Wood* (1920) and *The Use of Poetry and the Use of Criticism* (1933). In the same year as *A Christian Society* he published the light-verse collection *Old Possum's Book of Practical Cats* which, many years after its author's death, was to burst on to the London musical stage as the basis of the Andrew Lloyd Webber hit, *Cats*.

All of which hardly qualified him to speak as an expert on the subject of Christianity and social order, a fact which he readily acknowledged in his first chapter.

> This is a subject which I could, no doubt, handle much better were I a profound scholar in any of several fields. But I am not writing for scholars, but for people like myself; some defects may be compensated by some advantages; and what one must be judged by, scholar or no, is not particularised knowledge but one's total harvest of thinking, feeling, living and observing human beings.[58]

What Eliot provided was a discussion of what society might look like were a state to be 'arranged' according to Christian principles. He did not intend it to be a working blueprint for change, but a theoretical definition:

> I am not investigating the possible lines of action by which such a Christian society could be brought into being. I shall confine myself to a slight outline of what I conceive

58. T S Eliot, *The Idea of a Christian Society* (Faber and Faber, 1939), pp 7–8.

> to be essential features of this society, bearing in mind that it can neither be mediaeval in form, nor be modelled on the seventeenth century or any previous age. In what sense, if any, can we speak of a 'Christian State'? (p 25)

Almost immediately, Eliot makes a valuable caveat: 'The Christian and the unbeliever do not, and cannot, behave very differently in the exercise of office; for it is the general ethos of the people they have to govern, not their own piety, that determines the behaviour of politicians' (p 27). But he continues that 'it is not primarily the piety of the statesmen that matters, but their being confined, by the temper and traditions of the people by which they rule, to a Christian framework within which to realise their ambitions and advance the prosperity of their country'.

Thus Eliot adopts a similar position to that taken by Plato in *The Laws*, where a moral code defines the morality of government more than does the individual morality of its leaders. And if that body of morality were to be the biblical moral teachings, then the society so governed might be described as a Christian society. Yet he also affirms that rulers of a Christian society must be 'confined' to a Christian framework:

> The rulers . . . will, *qua* rulers, accept Christianity not simply as their own faith to guide their actions, but as the system under which they are to govern. The people will accept it as a matter of behaviour and habit.[59]

What would be needed, says Eliot, is a 'Community of Christians', formed of 'consciously and thoughtfully practising Christians', both laity and clergy. The relation of church and state in a Christian society would then have three elements:

> [The church] must have a hierarchical organisation in direct and official relation to the State: in which relation it is always in danger of sinking into a mere department

59. Ibid, p 35.

> of the State. It must have an organisation, such as the parochial system, in direct contact with the smallest units of the community and their individual members. And finally, it must have, in the persons of its more intellectual, scholarly and devout officers, its masters of ascetic theology and its men of wider interest, a relation to the Community of Christians.[60]

The Community would speak with final authority on matters of dogma, of faith and of morals. At times it would be in conflict with the State, defending its own rights and contesting heresy and immoral legislation. Sometimes the church would be under attack from the Community, for any organisation is 'always in danger of corruption and in need of reform from within'. The Community would in fact be the conscience of the nation.

For Eliot, attempting to define an idea and (in a sense) an ideal, it is self-evident that because the 'prevailing ethos' of a Christian state would be a Christian ethos, the government would be required to conform to Christian morals, and that the instrument of that conformity should be the Community of Christians. As with Plato, at the back of government stands a higher power, and in Eliot's Christian society the Community of Christians incarnates that higher power.

The Religious Basis of Society: Quintin Hogg

In 1947 Penguin Books commissioned two paperbacks: one by John Parker, *Labour Marches On*, and another by Quintin Hogg, *The Case For Conservatism*. Hogg, later Lord Chancellor as Lord Hailsham of Marylebone, produced a book that explored the political faith of his party at some length and considerable depth.

60. Ibid, p 47.

Hogg begins his second chapter, on 'The Religious Basis of Society', with the following assertion:

> I can discover no important writer on Conservatism who has not been driven to the same conclusion. There can be no genuine Conservatism which is not founded upon a religious view of the basis of civil obligation, and there can be no true religion where the basis of civil obligation is treated as purely secular.[61]

Hogg cites a range of authors – Burke, Disraeli, Winston Churchill – to illustrate his point, and makes three propositions: (a) that 'The spiritual brotherhood of mankind under the fatherhood of God is the sole philosophical justification for any sort of morality between man and man'; (b) that 'Religion provides the moral basis of culture without which man is unable to live at peace with his neighbour'; and (c) that 'I intend to develop some of the moral and political ideas which I hold as a Conservative. I begin by asserting all to be quite worthless except they are held and followed, in a religious way' (p 18).

He frames his argument very much in terms of the providence of God and the comforts and provisions of religion. But as he ends his chapter, Hogg defends God's 'policy' against those twentieth-century thinkers who would argue that events such as two world wars prove God's incompetence, 'as if He were a sort of universal Prime Minister'. On the contrary, he asserts,

> The policy . . . is well known. It is to tell human creatures of certain rules which they ought to follow – truthfulness, kindness, chastity, respect for parents, and, above all, worship of God, and to leave them more or less free to follow them or not (p 22).

Thus Hogg raises among his initial premises the fact that religion involves a responsibility and a response; that the beliefs you hold must necessarily produce some correlation

61. Quintin Hogg, *The Case for Conservatism* (Penguin, 1947), p 16.

in the way you behave; that there is therefore a link between public theology and private morality.

Certainly in the sphere of *public* morality he regards the powers of government as substantial. 'There is no sphere in which Government may not, in the name of the natural law, penetrate. There is no relationship, economic, social or even domestic, where legislation may not in some circumstances be appropriate to check, or even prevent, abuses' (p 54).

In his chapter on 'Authority' he is careful to point out that,

> Historically speaking, there is no reason to connect this process [a State's progress from barbarism to law and order] with the moral excellence or legitimist claims of the successful authority. (p 46).

He reminds us that the British Monarchy was established by conquest, that Menes did not unite the Kingdoms of Egypt because of 'any superiority in title or wisdom', that 'a popularly elected tyranny deserves no more respect than a self-appointed dictator'. What provides the stability and authority of government is 'natural law'. Discussing what this 'natural law' is, Hogg identifies a precept, 'disregard of which has caused much of the misery of our time': 'Thou shalt love thy neighbour as thyself.'

> In dealing with human beings, the means never justifies the end because each human soul is an ultimate in itself. The brotherhood of man is thus the basis of natural law, at once the basis and justification of all actual law in Britain and elsewhere (p 75).

It should be clear even from these extracts that Quintin Hogg was not arguing that because Conservatism is inconceivable without Christianity, all members of a Conservative administration must be Christians. He argued rather that a State should be moderated by a system of laws that reflects religious absolute truths; that for all citizens, being governed means subjecting themselves to the authority of that moral system in every area of life; and that the government was accountable according to the extent to which they implemented the religious/moral system.

The Two Cities: Lord Hailsham of Marylebone

Surprisingly, Quintin Hogg's 1947 study is not mentioned in the 1990 symposium, *Christianity and Conservatism*. It is surprising because the brief chapter contributed by Hogg, now Lord Hailsham, represents a continuation and development of his earlier argument.

Once again he emphasises the importance of loving one's neighbour, 'an individual, made in the image of God, and the individual so created is also a member of a vast number of different and overlapping associations, natural and voluntary, none of which is entitled to an absolute or undivided fealty'.[62]

He takes as his main reference Augustine's City of God. His chapter is entitled 'The Two Cities', and he makes a distinction between the *Civitas Deo* and the *Civitas terrena*. The City of God is a voluntary association, he points out, whereas the Earthly City is a natural society, which we do not choose to join and whose laws we are bound to obey. In the former City, there is no acceptable goal short of moral perfection. But the City of this world 'deals in sticks and carrots'. Presupposing a conventional morality, it is 'based on the art of the possible', and confined within the bounds of enforceability'. No parliament can force people to pray or to worship.

Yet there is a moral relationship, he insists, between the two cities. Nevertheless, this relationship cannot be interpreted as enforceable in either direction. As he said in 1947, you do not have to be a Christian to conform your governing to Christian standards. That being so, 'I doubt very much whether the professional clergy have very much of value to

62. Michael Alison and David L Edwards, eds, *Christianity and Conservatism* (Hodder & Stoughton, 1990), p 22.

add to the debate.' Very few political issues, he observes, have to do with the salvation of souls. He ends his chapter, 'In the *Civitas terrena*, the City of this world, we are all equals, and sky pilots should remember that if anything they are less equal than many others' (p 26).

Despite the irony of the last sentence, it is a strong argument. But it touches on an area which has been much argued over in modern apologetics. What does the Christian faith have to say about the secular world? Is there any part of life where Jesus is not Lord? And if politics is the pragmatic art of the possible, does Christianity have nothing to say about individual cases, having once set the moral agenda for stable government? In the arts, in social welfare, in many areas of life, the thrust of contemporary Christian apologetics has often been that the Bible is transformational, that a Christian doing art does it in some sense differently from an artist who is not a Christian. Does the Church really have so little to contribute of its own in politics?

Lord Hailsham demonstrated his position very well in a televised debate in January 1994, in which he was invited to comment on the press debate about public and government morality. His argument ran roughly as follows: 'If you ask me to speak as a Christian, then of course I want everybody to live by the moral standards of Jesus Christ. But if you ask me to speak as a *politician* . . .'

Are the two cities complementary and exclusive? Is there any case for one having a form of sovereignty over the other? If a minister enforces a Christian social code, does it matter if he or she breaks that code themselves?

Only, Lord Hailsham seems to say, in a marginal sense. For most of the time, the Christian code itself will preserve the moral health of the nation. In a similar way Plato argued that once having defined moral laws, they should never be changed, for in their existence and continuity the health of the popular soul lay.

A View from Canterbury : Archbishop William Temple

The 'Penguin Specials', of which Quintin Hogg's 1947 book formed part, were vehicles for some very widely-discussed views. One of the most successful, by the then Archbishop of York William Temple, was *Christianity and the Social Order* (1942). In the year it was published Temple became Archbishop of Canterbury. The book became an immediate best-seller and sold 139,000 copies.

> There were many who lacked convictions about the duty and place of the Church in the social life of the people, but were ready to listen to a case that might be put up for the 'interference' of the Church in the secular order; there was also a notable volume of opinion which vehemently denied that social and industrial problems came at all into the Church's legitimate scope of thought and action. At these two bodies, primarily, the 'Penguin' was aimed.[63]

Temple (1881–1944) was a philosopher by training, and as a churchman was ecumenical and interested in social issues (through the Workers' Educational Association) and in education (through the Student Christian Movement). He was a prominent spokesman in the affairs of the nation and contributed with other Christian church leaders to a Statement of Principles to guide a post-war settlement. He is often regarded as one of the fathers of the Welfare State, and spoke with the more authority, perhaps, because though a leader in the established church he argued cogently that the church and political parties should remain separate from each other.

In *Christianity and Social Order*, Temple argues a version of 'Back to Basics' of his own:

63. F A Iremonger, *William Temple, Archbishop of Canterbury: His Life and Letters* (OUP, 1948), p 435.

> It is wholesome to go back to the old conception of Natural Law because it holds together two aspects of truth which it is not easy to hold in combination – the ideal and the practical. We tend to follow one or other of two lines: either we start from a purely ideal conception, and then we bleat fatuously about love; or else we start from the world as it is with the hope of remedying an abuse here or there, and then we have no general direction or criterion of progress. The conception of Natural Law will help us to frame a conception of the right or ideal relation between the various activities of men and of the men engaged in them.[64]

Taking economics as an example of one of these 'activities', he explains that while economic processes can be isolated and run according to the self-sufficient laws of economics, to do so makes economics an end in itself – which it is not (p 58). It is a means, not an end; 'a means to the life of man'. If any activity of human beings is considered to be self-sufficient, then the Church must become involved, rebuking this 'dislocation of the structure of life' and if possible pointing out the way to recovery. As we have seen already (p 60), Temple argued that the Church should advocate principles rather than involving itself in technical areas of which it knew nothing. But for Temple, the Church is God's agent, by virtue of its nature and mission as the Body of Christ on earth, and because that is in any case the Church's traditional role until quite recent times (both reasons are discussed at length in his opening chapters).

It is a discussion rooted in values. In Chapter VII, 'The Task Before Us', Temple examines 'some of the principles by which the Christian tradition would lead us to direct human life' (p 62). Each value, if affirmed, would have immediate implications in everyday life. Holding that *The*

64. William Temple, *Christianity and Social Order* (Penguin, 1942), p 59.

Family is the Primary Social Unit would at once improve housing and leisure provision (Temple also mentions Sunday Trading. Christians affirming this and other biblical values were a considerable factor in the 1993–1994 Sunday Trading debates). The *Sanctity of Personality* would demand recognition that 'the supreme mark of a person is that he orders his life by his own deliberate choice'; and more than that, it would lead to improvements in public health – 'an undernourished and under-developed body is likely to house an irritable, querulous and defensive soul.' *The Principle of Fellowship* would promote educational values by which 'the best things possible to men' might be realised – Temple at this point advocated universal accessibility to education of all kinds – and would combat social snobbery, which he considered 'without parallel', and drudgery and insecurity in the workplace.

There had been an inversion of the natural order, argued the Archbishop; things had become ends in themselves, not ends to the life of man:

> If that is true, it is the duty of Christians to become aware of it and demand a remedy. It cannot be said that it is their duty as Christians to know what the remedy is, for this involves many technical matters. But they are entitled to call upon the Government to set before itself the following objectives and pursue them as steadily and as rapidly as opportunity permits. (p 73)

He proposed six objectives:

1. Every child should find itself a member of a family housed with decency and dignity . . .
2. Every child should have the opportunity of an education till years of maturity . . . This education should throughout be inspired by God and find its focus in worship . . .
3. Every citizen should be secure in possession of such income as will enable him to maintain a home and

bring up children in such conditions as are described in (1) above . . .

4. Every citizen should have a voice in the conduct of the business or industry which is carried on by means of his labour . . .
5. Every citizen should have sufficient daily leisure, with two days rest in seven and, if an employee, an annual holiday with pay . . .
6. Every citizen should have assured liberty in the forms of worship, of speech, of assembly, and of association for special purposes (pp 73–74).

It might seem at first sight that Temple is proposing a detailed agenda of specific steps. He is not; he is setting forth principles which can be applied in any situation (though in a personal appendix he outlines his own thoughts as to how they might be applied in 1942). The biblical nature of the principles is underlined by his final comments:

> This book is about Christianity and the Social Order, not about Evangelism. But I should give a false impression of my own convictions if I did not here add that there is no hope of establishing a more Christian social order except through the labour and sacrifice of those in whom the Spirit of Christ is active, and that the first necessity for progress is more and better Christians taking full responsibility as citizens for the political, social and economic system under which they and their fellows live (p 74).

Six Guiding Principles: The Movement for Christian Democracy

It is interesting to compare William Temple's six principles with the six 'Guiding Principles' outlined in the founding Westminster Declaration of the Movement for Christian

Democracy.[65] One of the founders of the movement, David Alton MP, discusses Temple with admiration in one of his books[66], and his thought is clearly part of the movement's heritage.

The Movement for Christian Democracy is not a political party but an all-party non-denominational Christian group, active at all political levels. Founded by MPs David Alton and Ken Hargreaves as a reaction to the politicisation of Christian ethics, it attacked the 'sidelining of basic Christian values'. David Alton has been a spokesman for a number of moral and ethical campaigns in Parliament, and his attempts to change the abortion law and the law on 'video nasties' have been influential.

The Declaration lists six 'guiding principles which highlight some basic themes of Christian Democracy'. They are: *Social justice* (as founded in the character of God and given by divine law); *Respect for life* (human beings are created in the image of God); *Reconciliation* (The kingdom of God is heralded by a community in which we are all to be reconciled in Jesus Christ); *Active compassion* (The God of justice is the God of love; we are called to active loving service of others); *Wise stewardship* (All economic activity involves our responsibility before God for the world entrusted to us); and *Empowerment* (Authority is given from God for the common good; those who have power are to be accountable).

The Declaration unpacks each of these. It is interesting to see how the emphases are similar to a number of other formulations, and the Declaration's intention not to promote a political manifesto but to make Christian values and Christian principles part of the political process. Temple believed that Christianity should be written into Government social policy; The Movement for Christian Democracy seeks to

65. Movement for Christian Democracy, 'The Westminster Declaration' (7-page A4 mimeograph, 17 November 1990).
66. David Alton, *Faith in Britain* (Hodder & Stoughton, 1991), pp 18–19.

unite Christian citizens in making Christian morality and perceptions a factor in political decisions by lobbying, discussing, interrogating candidates, and arguing the case in many other ways.

Because it is not a Christian political party the Movement is arguably better placed, as a pressure group, to raise the issues of Christian values. Some Christians in the past who have campaigned as 'Christian candidates' have found themselves marginalised by the leading parties' candidates, who all assured the electorate that they themselves fully endorsed Christian values; and as the Christian party candidate was invariably politically inexperienced, it would, the established parties argued, be a much better use of a vote to support *them*, the known and proven.

However, though the Movement itself would not become a political party, a party could well emerge from it. The Movement does not say it has the only Christian answer or approach to a particular issue: it would only claim, 'We are trying to marry biblical exegesis and principles with policy.' Scripture does not change, but policy develops. But in what political tradition would it grow? It would attempt to develop the best of British Christian roots and perspectives, but would acknowledge that Christian Democracy has a particularly Continental past. In that sense the Movement is attempting to import a foreign ideal to Britain, but to make it relevant to the domestic situation. The Movement for Christian Democracy is free to (and does) choose or reject from the mainland European tradition. It is not growing in a vacuum, but is confined by the traditions and principles of European Christian Democracy.[67]

67. I am grateful to David Campanale, of the Movement for Christian Democracy, for the substance of this paragraph and the preceding one. The European Christian Democratic tradition is discussed in David Alton, *Faith in Britain*, passim.

Behaving Christianly: C S Lewis

Though C S Lewis (1898–1963) had a wide popular readership for his books about Christianity, his world was the sheltered one of the university common room (his remarkable life and even more remarkable marriage have recently captured public imagination in the film *Shadowlands* and the stage play and television play of the same name that preceded it).

The topic of morality, both private and public, was one to which Lewis often turned. One of his most substantial discussions of the subject is to be found in *Christian Behaviour* (1943), which was to become part of *Mere Christianity* (1952). The centrality of moral absolutes in Lewis's theology is indicated by the fact that the first quarter of the latter book – one of the most (if not the most) influential popular apologetics for Christianity ever written – is devoted to the subject, and is entitled 'Right and Wrong as a Clue to the Meaning of the Universe'.

Lewis begins *Christian Behaviour* (a book almost contemporary with William Temple's *Christianity and Social Order*) by disabusing his readers of the notion that Christian morality is 'something that interferes, something that stops you having a good time'[68]. He defines it as concerned,

> Firstly, with fair play and harmony between individuals. Secondly, with what might be called tidying up or harmonising the things inside each individual. Thirdly, with the general purpose of human life as a whole: what man was made for.

Then, by way of a discussion of the seven Cardinal Virtues,

68. C S Lewis, *Christian Behaviour* (Bles, 1943). The unattributed quotations that follow are from the first chapter. It is interesting that Lewis chooses the word 'interferes', which is one Temple made much play on in his book which Lewis would probably have read while writing his own.

he rejects the idea that motives and manner were irrelevant to the moral acts one might perform; that God simply demands obedience to rules (he wants, says Lewis 'people of a particular sort'); and that virtue was a finite quality, for this world only and unnecessary in the next.

The consequence of these premises is that for Lewis, morality is not an autonomous private matter but has repercussions. He calls his second chapter 'Social Morality'. Morality, Lewis explains, means 'Do as you would be done by', and he explicitly concedes a notion of 'back to basics':

> As Dr Johnson said, 'People need to be reminded more often than they need to be instructed.' The real job of every moral teacher is to keep on bringing us *back*, time after time, to the old simple principles which we are all so anxious not to see . . .

(The italics are Lewis's.) He immediately adds that Christianity neither has nor should have a detailed political programme for applying moral principles to society; people who demand that the church should give a lead 'ought to mean the whole body of practising Christians', rather than wanting the clergy to preach a party line. The emphasis should be on the laity, all applying the principles of Christian morality to their own particular sphere of activity or place of work. 'All the same,' he adds,

> The New Testament, without going into details, gives us a pretty clear hint of what a fully Christian society would be like. Perhaps it gives us more than we can take. It tells us that there are to be no passengers or parasites: if a man doesn't work, he oughtn't to eat. Every one is to work with his own hands, and what is more, every one's work is to produce something good: there will be no manufacture of silly luxuries and then of sillier advertisements to persuade us to buy them. And there is to be no 'swank' or 'side', no putting on airs. To that extent a Christian society would be what we now call Leftist. On the other hand, it is always insisting on obedience –

> obedience (and outward marks of respect) from all of us to properly appointed magistrates, from children to parents, and (I'm afraid this is going to be very unpopular) from wives to husbands. Thirdly, it is to be a cheerful society: full of singing and rejoicing, and regarding worry and anxiety as wrong.[69]

It's an attractive picture, not least for its third point. But Lewis immediately points out that such a society, were we to visit it, would seem at once advanced (for its socialist-flavoured economy) and old-fashioned. Very few would like it in its entirety. Most people would like parts of it but not the whole, for it is in the nature of Christianity, Lewis suggests, that people take what they like and reject the rest, so that often two people's definition of Christianity can be markedly different.

He completes his discussion of social morality by questioning the principle of investment – 'lending money at interest' – as the basis of our economic system; he confesses his lack of expertise in economics, but points out that three great civilisations appear to have condemned that very thing. And he talks about charity as an inseparable part of Christian morality, whether or not the society in which it is practised already makes provision for the needy.

Lewis was writing in 1943, and his attitudes have sometimes dated along with his public-school slang (which George Orwell detested; and ridiculed him for, in reviewing *Mere Christianity*). But in *Christian Behaviour* he characteristically puts his finger on some key points that are central to the contemporary debate. Lewis's analysis can be summarised as follows.

First, *There is a core of Christian behavioural and moral standards, from which society has departed and to which it ought to return.* This sounds quite straightforward, but Lewis roots it in a complex reality. Personal and public moral standards

69. Ibid, p 18.

relate to the absolute moral character of God. Christian behaviour ultimately requires a relationship to him. Back to basics, therefore, means back to God.

Second, *Morality is more than duty and cannot be satisfied by mere observance.* A significant part of the book is the discussion of charity mentioned above. The 'basics' are not a matter of governments being effective providers, but of people sacrificially giving more than they can spare. In other words, adequate state provision never relieves individuals of the moral necessity for charity. In the modern context this might be translated into the concept of compassion: a society that institutes a system of social benefits is still not a moral society unless there is some sense of caring and even of moral outrage that anybody should be disadvantaged.

Third, *The church must lead as a group of individuals, not as a monolithic block voter.* At one level Lewis is merely explaining that the varied personality of the church and the breadth of interpretation that is inevitable, and also the undesirability of the church appearing to have a 'party line' in political debate, make it necessary that the church be speaking as a group of individuals rather than as a single voice. But along with this practical *modus operandi*, there is a deeper theme; that of the church as a vast transforming influence in society, each person bringing Christian morality to bear on his or her situation, affecting national life at a grass-roots as well as a board-room level.

Fourth, *To be morally observant is to be personally and spiritually fulfilled.* Lewis's worry-free, singing society is not complacent or naive. Its happiness is itself moral, for it regards worry and anxiety as wrong. And if that is so, then to cause worry and anxiety must be wrong too; so Lewis turns the responsibility for social happiness back on to those who govern society. But,

Fifthly, *Though government must lead a moral society, it is the people who make it moral.* 'A Christian society is not going to arrive until most of us really want it,' says Lewis (p 20), 'and we are not going to want it until we become fully Christian:'

> I may repeat 'Do as you would be done by' till I am black in the face, but I can't really carry it out till I love my neighbour as myself: and I can't learn to love my neighbour as myself till I learn to love God: and I can't learn to love God except by learning to obey Him.

So, concludes Lewis, it is necessary to look within ourselves, from social concerns to religious ones. Unlike Lord Hailsham, for whom moral laws provide social morality whoever administers them, for C S Lewis the morality of society seems inextricably bound up with the necessity for people to be moral – not only in order to fitly administer the state, but also because that is what God requires of all individuals.

Moral Code, Moral Law: Dorothy L Sayers

The question of moral leadership of nations is rarely so clearly argued as at times of war, when politicians hone their rhetoric and theologians frequently find that the academic issues of the university common room have become surprisingly relevant. Somebody who had a foot in both camps was the influential Christian writer Dorothy L Sayers.

Admired by C S Lewis's circle, Sayers (1893–1957) like Lewis gained a wide reputation as a populariser of Christianity, most effectively through the cycle of radio plays *The Man Born to be King* (1942) which she wrote for the BBC. Her controversial use of colloquial speech and her idiomatic treatment of biblical themes secured her a large listening audience. Like Lewis too, she was a successful writer of fiction. Her books about the aristocratic detective Lord Peter Wimsey remain in print and have been dramatised and filmed. She did not achieve the extraordinary success as an apologist for Christianity that Lewis did, but her audience was a large one and books such as *The Mind of the Maker* (1941) and *Unpopular Opinions* (1946) are still read. Her academic ability, obvious in the sometimes rather over-erudite detective stories (J R R Tolkien said Wimsey 'made him sick'), was demonstrated best in her influential translation of Dante, left incomplete at her death.

Sayers is interesting in the present discussion, though she touches on our subject only obliquely in her writing. She frequently portrayed Britain as a kind of moral guardian of the West, as for example in a letter to the Canadian Prime Minister during the Second World War:

> For nearly nine hundred years we have kept the gate of Europe open. . . . Yet, when we saw the enemy in the Channel Ports, we felt a great lifting of the heart, because then we knew for a certainty that what people had been saying about us was not true. We knew again who we were, and what we were for . . . [70]

This certainly ascribes the duty of morality to government, but it is not one of Sayers' most convincing pieces of writing and is little more than conventional wartime rhetoric such as is found in the pamphlets of Lord Vansittart and other wartime propagandists.

She is much more interesting on the same subject in an essay written in 1943 entitled 'They Tried to be Good'[71], in which she responds to criticisms of British inter-war policy and discusses contemporary war policy, with a typically strong irony and more than a dash of rhetoric. She argues that the whole sorry history of British government appeasement is because the British people 'want to be good'. She defines this as a childlike longing for divine, 'parental approval', and says that the corollary is also true: 'If they feel themselves to be naughty and in disgrace, they lose

70. Letter of 12 May 1944, quoted in: Barbara Reynolds, *Dorothy L Sayers: Her Life and Soul* (Hodder & Stoughton, 1993), p 351.
71. Collected in: Dorothy L Sayers, *Unpopular Opinions* (Gollancz, 1946), p 97.

self-confidence and develop inferiority psychoses; everything they do goes wrong.'

The lamentable recent history of Britain, she argues, is the result of 'the Voice of Enlightenment' assuring the British people that everything they had been doing was 'naughty'. The First World War, for example: 'a just war was as wicked as an unjust war'. The Voice, adds Sayers, reinforced itself 'with all the numinous authority of the Sermon on the Mount and all the persuasive reasonableness of Progressive Humanism. Britain listened, and tried to be good.' Britain was similarly troubled by the use of power to keep peace, by the naughtiness of Empire and possessions and self-interest, and by sentiment.

It was the Voice of Enlightenment, continued Sayers, that said that the vanquished foe of 1914–1918 must be brought into a peace partnership with the victors. But, she observes,

> Of course, when one takes a former foe into partnership, it is because one is convinced that he, too, 'wants to be good'. Germany, it now seems, did not want to be good, and Britain ought to have known it. But all the good and intellectual people who preached Progressive Humanism had been proclaiming for years that nobody ever wants to be naughty. There were no sinful men; indeed, there was no such thing as sin. There were only fundamentally good and perfectible men thwarted by oppressive circumstances. Take away the unfavourable environment, and everyone would at once be good and co-operate for the happiness of all.[72]

But, Sayers points out, the same Enlightened people who proclaimed that war was naughty also urged Britain to intervene in other nation's warring naughtiness. 'In one sphere after another, action stultified itself', as the principle of self-determination produced innumerable and horribly complicated moral dilemmas.

72. Ibid, p 99.

Hitler's appearance complicated matters still further, for he argued that 'his German-speaking minorities all over the world had the right to self-determination, even if this meant breaking up political and territorial units such as Czecho-Slovakia'. Frontiers, like war, were 'naughty'. But eventually, when Hitler demanded peoples and places that were not German and did not want to be German, it was reluctantly concluded that Germany – 'there was no help for it' – must be wicked too and that war must be declared.

'Britain slunk into war', observes Sayers dryly, 'with her tail between her legs, ground down by a vivid sense of her irredeemable naughtiness . . .' Repeatedly Britain's conduct of the war was criticised as 'naughty', and she was too dispirited to retort that the Voice of Enlightenment had sapped her will and burdened her with inferiority.

Until, that is, the moment when Hitler's war machine had stormed its way across Europe and stood at the Channel Ports. 'And Britain, stripped naked in the arena to await the pounce of the beast, was aware of a strange quality in the silence. *The scolding had stopped*. . . . We were not [considered] naughty any more.'

Sayers likened the arrival of Churchill to the arrival – after the departure of a peevish nanny – of a tart, bustling, comfortable Old Nurse 'who knew our family ways'. Churchill was corporeal and obstinately unenlightened. His theology was 'coarse and Christian enough to allow for sin and the devil, and sufficiently Pelagian (in the English manner) to admit the possibility of salvation by works'. He approved of what the Voice of Enlightenment disapproved of. 'He lived in the present, according to the Gospel of St. Matthew, instead of the next era but two, according to the Gospel of St. Marx.' He assumed that the British were 'all his sort of person' and told the Axis so.

> Now I should not dream of asserting that we were, or are, or ever shall be good as gold. All men are sinners, and the British are no exception. But I do say that we tried to

> be good. Our worst betrayals, our most flagrant stupidities resulted from our efforts to obey the contradictory orders of the silliest nursery governess ever foisted on a well-meaning bunch of children. I have no use whatever for Enlightened Opinion, whose science is obsolete, its psychology superficial, its theology beneath contempt and its history nowhere; besides, it is a craven thing . . . [73]

The core of Sayers' case comes in her closing paragraph, on the reason for Britain's 'decades of disaster'. 'We wanted to be good and tried to be good, but . . . the sincerest efforts after virtue produce only chaos if they are directed by a ramshackle and incoherent philosophy.'

Sayers wrote extensively during the war years. She argued that the church should not become identified with politics, for its kingdom was not of this world. She saw her times as being threatened by the disintegration of all that was to be cherished. She argued that though the church should not be *uninterested* in the social, political and moral sphere of the Law, it must be *disinterested*.[74] Her point in 'They Tried to be Good' is that political leaders had directed the people with a philosophy that fell far short of the truth; had they allowed themselves to be guided in their own turn by the truth – as Churchill was guided, she argues, though he was not a spiritual leader as such – they would have guided the nation into an earlier moral stance.

In another book, *The Mind of the Maker* (1941), Sayers discussed the difference between a moral law and a moral code. Moral codes are merely human formulations; moral laws are fixed and unalterable. 'The Mosaic Law is not in itself the moral law. Unlike the moral law, it does not have an absolute claim regardless of those to whom it is addressed. It is a modification of the moral law relating to the "hardness

73. Ibid, p 105.
74. Barbara Reynolds, op cit, p 337.

of men's hearts".'[75] Thus, argues Sayers, the cricketing authorities could change the rules of cricket if they so wished, to have seven players on each side; but what they cannot do is to decree that the ball must be hit in such a way that it never comes down again.[76] It is the sense of being subject to moral laws that the Voices of Enlightenment lacked, in Sayers's estimation. Their moral codes were inadequate.

In terms of our discussion so far, Dorothy L Sayers argues strongly that if the leaders of the nation make themselves accountable to a higher moral authority, the nation will act morally.

Double Listening: John Stott

For many Christians, general statements like those above have an air of unreality as they contemplate the law of Britain and find it often at odds with what they take to be biblical teaching. How *precisely* should a Christian respond, for example, to legislation that permits shops to trade on Sundays in the same way that they do on other days of the week – and to discriminate against people who cannot work on Sunday for religious reasons? How exactly does one go about persuading the leaders of the nation to act morally?

It's a theme that all the writers mentioned in this chapter discuss to varying degrees, the task of translating ideas into deeds. A contemporary writer who has done much to stimulate evangelical thinking about Christian involvement in social and political issues is John Stott. He was Founder of, was for several years Director of, and is now President of, Christian Impact, the study centre in London's West End. His books are read world-wide; they include commen-

75. John Peck, *Wisdom in the Marketplace: God's Wisdom for a Confused World* (Greenbelt Festivals, 1989), p 47.
76. Dorothy L Sayers, *The Mind of the Maker* (Methuen, 1941), chapter 1.

taries, apologetics, theological works and Bible reading aids. He is Rector Emeritus of All Soul's Church, Langham Place, and has had an extensive ministry among students. All of which meant that by the time he came to write two substantial books on Christianity and current secular issues, the books were destined to have a very wide influence indeed.

Issues Facing Christians Today (1984) was written in response to a 'half-century of neglect' by evangelicals of the conviction that:

> God has given us social as well as evangelistic responsibilities in his world. Yet the half-century of neglect has put us far behind in this area. We have a long way to catch up. This book is my own contribution to the catching up process.[77]

Seen by its author as a sister volume to the 1984 work, *The Contemporary Christian* (1992) contains 'twenty-one chapters about our present Christian responsibilities'. It relates 'to questions of doctrine and discipleship under the five headings "The Gospel", "The Disciple", "The Bible", "The Church" and "The World".'[78] Both books have extremely helpful historical chapters describing Christian involvement over the past decades, though these are often restricted to evangelical history – understandably, as both books are written as challenges to evangelicals.

A central element in *The Contemporary Christian* is John Stott's emphasis on 'double listening', which Christians are called to practise instead of the 'double refusal' of escapism into the Bible and conformity to the world. Double listening means listening both to the Word and to the world. The former, says Stott, is more congenial to us than the latter; but,

77. John Stott, *Issues Facing Christians Today* (Marshalls, 1984), p xi.
78. John Stott, *The Contemporary Christian: An Urgent Plea for Double Listening* (IVP, 1992), p 12.

> It is only through the discipline of double listening that it is possible to become a 'contemporary Christian'. For then we see that the adjectives 'historical' and 'contemporary' are not incompatible, we learn to apply the Word to the world, and we proclaim good news which is both true and new. In sum, we live in the 'now' in the light of the 'then'.[79]

The Contemporary Christian is a substantial book of 432 pages, which will not be summarised here. The five key questions that he addresses are significant. To quote the publisher's description on the back cover, summarising Stott's theme:

> Amid scepticism inside the church as well as outside, *what is the authentic gospel?*
> In a world torn by pain and need, *what characterizes the obedient disciple?*
> Now that the Bible is often set aside as culturally irrelevant, *how can we relate it with integrity to contemporary society?*
> Given the church's general lack of credibility, *what is her calling and how can she fulfil it?*
> In a pluralistic society and a hungry world, *what is the church's mission?*

It adds up to a programme of social action, though one quite different from what may have been looked for. A Christian cannot make a difference just by looking closely at the world and seeing its needs. Neither can he or she make a difference just by immersing themselves in the Bible. But when they do both, Christians will be well placed, says John Stott, to know precisely what to do to make a difference; for their understanding will have been sharpened by their listening to the world, and their vocation, their being guided by God, their empowering by his Spirit will be all the sharper by their listening to the Word.

79. Ibid, p 29.

5

THE BIBLICAL CASE: SOME KEY PASSAGES

With John Stott's plea for double listening fresh in our mind, we turn now to look briefly at some key passages in the Bible that are relevant to our topic.

The historical argument of which we have seen a number of examples going back as far as Plato, that behind the governors and leaders of states is an absolute morality to which they themselves are subject, found a Christian spokesman in Samuel Rutherford (c1600–1661), a Scottish Presbyterian whose chequered academic career culminated in his appointment to the chair of divinity at St Mary's College, St Andrews, where he became principal in 1647.

Rutherford took the Scottish Presbyterian cause to London, being one of eight Scottish Commissioners at the 1643 Westminster Assembly. In 1644 he published *Lex Rex: A Dispute for the Just Prerogative of King and People*. This book, which was a critique of absolute monarchy, made him a well-known political theorist. Among his later works *A Free Disputation against Pretended Liberty of Conscience* (1648) opposed religious toleration on the grounds that it put the human conscience in place of God and the Bible. At the Restoration of 1660, *Lex Rex* was outlawed and publicly burned and its author condemned to death by the Scottish

Parliament. Rutherford died before the sentence could be carried out.

Lex Rex means 'The Law is King', and by its very title defies the ancient theory of the Divine Right of Kings. According to Rutherford, kings *are* answerable to the same absolute moral law as their subjects. If they fail to satisfy that law, then they lose the right to be obeyed and the right to rule. Divine Right had claimed that the king was God's regent on earth; *Lex Rex* claimed this would be to put monarchy above the law to which it ought to submit. For Rutherford, arguing from Romans 13, monarchy and state existed only to incarnate God's law and govern their people according to the law of God. If the state committed any act that was contrary to God's law it was behaving tyrannically and should be disobeyed.

Somebody who did much to popularise Rutherford in the 1980s was Francis Schaeffer, who quoted Rutherford in his *Christian Manifesto* (1981):

> Rutherford held that a tyrannical government is always immoral. He said that 'a power ethical, politic, or moral, to oppress, is not from God, and is not a power, but a licentious deviation of a power; and is no more from God, but from sinful nature and the old serpent, than a license to sin.'[80]

Schaeffer summarises Rutherford as follows:

> Rutherford presents several arguments to establish the right and duty of resistance to unlawful government. *First*, since tyranny is satanic, not to resist it is to resist God – to resist tyranny is to honor God. *Second*, since the ruler is granted power conditionally, it follows that the people have the power to withdraw their sanction if the proper conditions are not fulfilled. The civil magistrate is a 'fiduciary figure' – that is, he holds his authority in trust for

80. Francis A Schaeffer, *A Christian Manifesto* (USA: Crossway, 1981), p 100.

> the people. Violation of the trust gives the people a legitimate base for resistance. It follows from Rutherford's thesis that citizens have a *moral* obligation to resist unjust and tyrannical government.[81]

Schaeffer was writing about civil disobedience, but Rutherford's arguments were general ones and directly bear upon our subject; a ruler who fails according to the moral law has failed in his task of ruling well, and the people have failed morally too if they do not resist him.

Rutherford was careful to say that isolated acts of immorality and occasional misdemeanours do not justify removing a ruler from office or a programme of civil disobedience. The point at which that is necessary is when the very fabric of society has been corrupted by the behaviour of its leaders. Even in a period such as that in 1993–1994, in which a succession of leading politicians and senior government officers were publicly exposed as moral failures, it would be difficult to argue that Rutherford's point of no return had been reached. However, his insistence on the supremacy of the law above the government makes him a good starting point for a brief examination of some key biblical passages on our subject, and we begin with a passage on which Rutherford based a good deal of his political thought.

Romans 13

> Paul places the whole question on a very high plane. God Himself is the fount of all authority, and those who exercise authority on earth do so by delegation from Him; therefore to disobey them is to disobey God. . . . But what if the authorities themselves are unrighteous?[82]

This chapter has traditionally been a problem, for it can be

81. Ibid, p 101.
82. F F Bruce, *Romans: An Introduction and Commentary* (IVP Tyndale Press, 1963), p 233.

interpreted in various ways. It can be understood, for example, to mean that Christians should obey without question whatever government is in power over them. But there are passages in Scripture where this is clearly contradicted: the apostles in Acts 17:6–7, for instance, and the example of Jesus himself who on several occasions made it clear that he did not regard himself as bound to obey the authorities unquestioningly. Rutherford's argument would suggest that there are circumstances in which rulers can forfeit the respect of Christians. H C G Moule succinctly remarks,

> The passage assumes, of course, that where human law, or its minister, contradicts divine precepts, (as when a Christian is commanded to do wrong,) then obedience to the Higher Authority must take precedence.[83]

What then does verse 1 mean? Manfred Brauch warns,

> If we cannot give uncritical and unquestioning allegiance to the demands of society and its governing authorities, we must also be careful not to go to the other extreme, that of concluding that government is inevitably an evil institution which should be resisted, disobeyed, distrusted or ignored.[84]

In between these extremes, two comments on this chapter are particularly helpful in the present discussion. The first is Karl Barth's suggestion that the words 'submit himself' (13:1) actually have to do with how we think about government. It means seeing rulers as God sees them, by which change of perspective the earthly powers and authorities are radically redefined:

> It is evident that there can be no more devastating undermining of the existing order than the recognition of it

83. H C G Moule, *The Epistle of Paul the Apostle to the Romans . . .* (C.U.P., 1879), p 215.
84. Manfred T Brauch, *Hard Sayings of St Paul* (Hodder & Stoughton, 1990), p 81.

> which is here recommended, a recognition rid of all illusion and devoid of all the joy of triumph.[85]

The second is Manfred Brauch's suggestion firstly that rulers are part of God's plan for bringing about his intent of harmony and order in community life, and that they therefore lose the right to be obeyed when they depart from this; and secondly that the passage is really about caring for others in love.[86]

Across a wide range of opinions there is considerable agreement that if politicians behave immorally or encourage immoral behaviour in those they lead, they have forfeited the respect to which, under God, they are entitled.

1 Peter 2:13–14

> Submit yourselves for the Lord's sake to every authority instituted among men: whether to the king, as the supreme authority, or to governors, who are sent by him to punish those who do wrong and to commend those who do right.

This passage is the more striking because Peter was probably writing while Nero was emperor. Does this mean that even the most inhuman regime deserves obedience? The difficulties of a particular British government facing a succession of moral catastrophes would seem very insignificant compared to the gross excesses of Nero's court. And how does the immorality of Nero's entourage square with the description of earthly rulers as God's moral watchdogs?

According to several commentators, the key to understanding this passage is to see it in terms not of the relationship between Christians and rulers, but between Christians and the watching world. In any society, the rules of behaviour

85. Karl Barth tr Edwyn C Hoskyns, *The Epistle to the Romans* (OUP, 1933), p 483.
86. Manfred T Brauch, op cit, pp 82–84.

are set by the ruling authorities. Christians should be doubly careful to submit to any moral or ethical laws and regulations, because if they do not they will bring the name of Christ into disrepute and become known as immoral people. 'The Jews were especially hated and counted infamous for this reason,' observes John Calvin, 'because they were regarded on account of their perverseness as ungovernable.'[87] In the old Communist bloc, though religious freedom was minimal, there were many regulations on everyday morality and behaviour. Frequently these were trivial and irksome and many citizens ignored them, but in Peter's terms they were to be meticulously obeyed.

Revelation 13 and 18

These passages are mentioned here because they once again encourage a different perspective. Often governments are unjust and unfair, and obeying them is frustrating and difficult. It is possible to become voluntarily redundant and make more money from state benefits than from one's salary while employed. Young people can be condemned to long-term unemployment, and often see government training schemes as cynical. Sometimes it seems that there is no point in working, and those who have worked hard all their lives often find when they retire that they are far worse off than they expected. What makes it worse is that those who cheat the system seem to be doing so well out of it. In such circumstances a Christian may well be tempted to reject any idea of being submissive to the government that has allowed such things to happen and in some cases has caused them to happen by its policies. Governments can be guilty of structural sin and immorality, for which they are jointly responsible; is that kind of immorality to be tolerated, while personal immorality is dragged through the tabloids?

It's not only a modern problem. In biblical times people

87. John Calvin, *On the First Epistle of Peter*, comment on 2:14.

faced the same difficulties. On every hand, in generation after generation there was corruption, graft, cruelty and immorality. Asaph recorded it in poetry:

> But as for me, my feet had almost slipped;
> I had nearly lost my foothold.
> For I envied the arrogant
> when I saw the prosperity of the wicked. . . .
> This is what the wicked are like –
> always carefree, they increase in wealth.
> Surely in vain have I kept my heart pure;
> in vain have I washed my hands in innocence.
> All day long I have been plagued;
> I have been punished every morning.
> If I had said, 'I will speak thus,'
> I would have betrayed your children.[88]

For Asaph it all seemed too much, until he changed his perspective:

> When I tried to understand all this,
> it was oppressive to me
> till I entered the sanctuary of God;
> then I understood their final destiny. (vv 16–17)

The apocalyptic doom of Revelation 13, which shows the state become a tool of Satan, and Revelation 18, which portrays the destruction of the great city of Babylon, remind us that states and governments do come under the judgement of God. The functions they are allowed to exercise they exercise by his forbearance, and in the perspective of history any injustices and immorality will not go unpunished.

We live, as Augustine reminds us, in two cities at once. The calling of Christians is to be sure where their primary allegiance lies and on which future their eyes are fixed.

88. Psalm 73:2–3,12–16.

The ancient values

In the Bible, the past is important.

> 'Stand at the crossroads and look;
> ask for the ancient paths,
> ask where the good way is, and walk in it,
> and you will find rest for your souls.
> But you said, "We will not walk in it." '[89]

The Israelites are constantly told to look back to their historic experiences; the years of slavery, the Exodus, the desert years, the wars that God had led them through, the prophets he had sent to them, the miracles.

This use of the past is quite different from the various uses of it we have seen in this book so far, however. There is no wistfulness, no sense that it was all much better then and perhaps it would be a good idea to recreate that vanished golden age. Bible characters compare the present ungodliness to happier times, but the emphasis is on the present and the future. History is moving forward.

The reason is twofold. Firstly, of course, the sense of the forward dynamic in history is very strong in the Bible. The linear direction is from creation through fall through atonement to redemption, and the vanished glories of Eden will be forgotten in the vaster glories of the New Jerusalem. In the Bible story, nobody who really understands what is happening is very interested in the past as an ideal.

But, secondly, they *are* interested in the past, but for a different reason. The past is their proof of the goodness of God. He reminds them of that fact constantly. 'Remember . . . that the Lord your God brought you out of [Egypt] with a mighty hand and an outstretched arm' (Deuteronomy 5:15), he says, sounding a note that is repeated throughout the Old Testament. But even this appeal to the past is in the context of a future certainty:

89. Jeremiah 6:16.

> I am the Lord; that is my name!
> I will not give my glory to another
> or my praise to idols.
> See, the former things have taken place,
> and new things I declare;
> before they spring into being
> I announce them to you.[90]

What such passages indicate is that the Bible has no place for wistful nostalgia. The past is important because it speaks about the character and faithfulness of God. The old values are God's values, but his expectation is that they will be renewed every day, not admired longingly from a distance. Nor does the Bible draw up lists of values to which believers are invited to return. The values that are important are generated by the encounter between human beings and God. Though a community of believers, because they have the same God, will have many values in common, this does not mean that there is anything stereotyped about the values of the kingdom.

90. Isaiah 42:8–9.

6

THE VALUES OF THE NEW SOCIETY

Let us now bring together some of the strands we have been examining. We began by identifying two questions that are often asked today: first, are there moral values with which our society has lost touch and to which we ought to be trying to return? And second, does a moral society require moral leaders? If so, what is the responsibility of citizens, and Christian citizens in particular, when the government or its officers are discovered to have acted immorally?

If we are looking for Christian values, a good place to start is the early church in the Book of Acts, meeting in the knowledge of the resurrection and with the light of the New Testament morning in its eyes. Luke presents us with what is, in terms of the Christian church, something of a golden age.

> They devoted themselves to the apostles' teaching and to the fellowship, to the breaking of bread and to prayer. Everyone was filled with awe, and many wonders and miraculous signs were done by the apostles. All the believers were together and had everything in common. Selling their possessions and goods, they gave to anyone as he had need. Every day they continued to meet together in the temple courts. They broke bread in their homes

> and ate together with glad and sincere hearts, praising God and enjoying the favour of all the people.
> (Acts 2:42–47)

> All the believers were one in heart and mind. No-one claimed that any of his possessions was his own, but they shared everything they had. With great power the apostles continued to testify to the resurrection of the Lord Jesus, and much grace was upon them all. There were no needy persons among them. For from time to time those who owned lands or houses sold them, brought the money from the sales and put it at the apostles' feet, and it was distributed to anyone as he had need.
> (Acts 4:32–35)

It is perhaps one of the most astonishing paradoxes of the early church that at the point that it was at its most doctrinally pure it was also most effective practically. Where it was nearest to heaven, it was most securely grounded in earthly reality. This was no forced communism, as Acts 4 shows, expanding upon Acts 2. There is an almost laconic tone to that 'from time to time'; as if, so soon as somebody became aware of a need, his or her immediate response was to decide what of their own they could sell. 'Possessions' were thus transformed from encumbrances to assets to be used, either by liquidating them or by sharing them. The sin of Ananias and Sapphira related in the following chapter was not that they retained part of their property, but that they pretended they had given it all. The hallmark of that little society was not that everybody had the same, but that none were in need. Speaking of the early church, Michael Green has said,

> The message of the Kingdom became more than an idea. A new human community had sprung up and looked very much like the new order to which the evangelist had pointed. Here love was given daily expression; reconciliation was actually occurring; people were no longer

> divided into Jew and Gentile, slave and free, male and female. In the community the weak were protected, the stranger welcomed. People were healed, the poor and dispossessed were cared for and found justice. Everything was shared. Joy abounded and ordinary lives were filled with praise.[91]

It would be difficult to devise a more impressive list of 'basic values'. To identify a few of them: the early Christians lived by love, by reconciliation, by ethnic tolerance, by social equality, by the dignity both of men and of women, by compassion for the disadvantaged, by help for the weak, by justice, mercy, and generosity of purse and spirit. The result was a huge increase in credibility and 'the favour of the people'. History records that this popular approval was short-lived, for the message of the cross brought confrontation and hostility. Many of those who shared in that halcyon fellowship would find themselves before very long scorned and hated; some would be imprisoned, tortured and even executed for their faith. Indeed, in view of the history of persecution that the young church was about to experience, one might wonder why there was that initial popularity at all.

The reason was simply that no objective eyewitness could deny the contrast between the corporate life of the church and the values by which secular society of the day was ordered. 'The practical application of charity was probably the most potent single cause of Christian success,' observes Henry Chadwick. 'The pagan comment "See how these Christians love one another" (reported by Tertullian) was not irony.'[92] The little group not only cared for its own members in a situation of increasing hostility from outsiders,

91. Michael Green, quoted in Jim Wallis, *The Call to Conversion: Recovering the Gospel for These Times* (USA: Harper & Row, 1981), p 15. I owe this reference to Michael Marshall, *The Gospel Conspiracy* (Monarch, 1992), p 177.
92. Henry Chadwick, *The Early Church* (Penguin, 1967), p 57.

it provided a demonstration of values to the world in which it existed.

To many who were part of the church it must have seemed like heaven on earth. Many – not least the women – came from societies where they had never been conceded full human rights. Many had been slaves, many still were; many had been poor, many still were. Some, no doubt, were categorised by their old world as socially stigmatised, for example because of mental or physical disability. Now all that was changed. Nobody was in need. Nobody thought that anybody else was an inferior person to him or herself. All followed a risen Lord who had treated women as social equals, who had broken innumerable social taboos, had ridiculed shibboleths, and had not been afraid to accuse contemporary religious leaders of dead observances and repressive legalism.

Looking back over 2,000 years, the picture in Acts loses none of its wonder and appeal. And unlike the utopias we have already considered in Chapter One, it is neither theoretically unrealistic nor unworkable. The picture given in Acts 2 and 4 is, quite simply, a picture of the normal Christian society. Though Christianity through the ages has fallen consistently short of the ideal and has tempered the purity of the gospel model, and though the name of Christianity has sometimes been disgraced throughout history by societies and individuals who took the name 'Christian' but had no allegiance to Christ, the model endures. In this sense a society based on Christian values *is* possible. The only proviso is that it must of necessity always be a world within the world.

It must be so, because no human state or nation has a wholly Christian population. Even in Mizoram and Nagaland, the predominantly Christian Indian states we have already considered, there are immigrant communities, foreign transients and a number of people who have not become Christians. The Christian society described in Acts presupposes that every member of it shares the same commitment to each other and to Jesus Christ. While it must have appeared a gracious and winsome society to those who visited from outside, such visitors could have shared in the joys and happiness of the society only if they became members of it. In that most outward-looking of communities, here was no room for outsiders. There is no possibility of recreating it, therefore, in terms of the modern state. The reason is not because of human and civil rights, of the need to respect the rights of those who belong to other religions or to none at all. It is because love cannot be coerced. In a society where any people at all do not love Jesus Christ, and therefore their brothers and sisters too, the miracle of the young church cannot be created afresh as a national pattern of government.

Yet it *is* recreated, in every church and every fellowship where the New Testament rule of love is practised, whether literally or symbolically, as a practical outworking of the theological truth that the church is the body of Jesus Christ on earth. And it is in such places that the church best provides what Peter Baelz[93] calls a symbolic pattern of government. In other words, the church provides a model of values not primarily because of the truth to which it holds but because of the lifestyle to which it is called. It preaches its doctrines by proclamation, but it preaches its values by example.

Perhaps those of us who long for a Christian state have missed the point in our fallen world. The Christian society exists wherever two or three are gathered in Christ's name and seek to live the gospel way. The values that so marked out the early church were their values because they held Jesus to be central and they were unashamedly living for God in the power of his Spirit. Wherever people do the same today, those values are generated afresh.

93. See the quotation in Chapter 1 (p 41), footnoted 25.

The source of kingdom values

But what is the church *for*? Is it to be just a holy huddle, bolstering up each other's unworldly faith, caring for each other and fostering godly values in a cloistered and secluded environment? By no means.

In his final discourse with the disciples before he went to Gethsemane and on to Calvary, Jesus told them what the future held for them – and for everybody who would ever become a Christian, the church of Jesus Christ through history (John 17:20). Many themes were covered in that lengthy discourse, among them the following.

The church is not to be afraid

'Remain in my love,' he said (15:9). How? By obedience to his commands. And it is always primary in Jesus' teaching about what life would be like for them after he had gone back to his Father, that none of them would enjoy an idyllic, super-spiritual existence. Remaining in his love meant remaining his associate, sharing his ministry and sharing his troubles.

They were to remain in his love. It is a love shared by a community that was wholly dedicated to each other, but a community that was following a great example. 'Love each other as I have loved you. Greater love has no-one than this, that he lay down his life for his friends' (vv 12–13). Throughout the discourse, Jesus makes clear that the security of the church lies not in the quality but in the source of its mutual love. For example: 'If the world hates you, keep in mind that it hated me first' (v 18); 'The Father himself loves you because you have loved me and have believed that I came from God' (16:27); and the breathtaking, blazingly confident guarantee of 16:33 – 'I have told you these things, so that in me you may have peace. In this world you will have trouble. But take heart! I have overcome the world.'

The promise of peace is a consequence of the centrality

of God and the triumph of his Son. Faith in Jesus Christ is both a means and a condition of that peace.

> Do not let your hearts be troubled. Trust in God; trust also in me. In my Father's house are many rooms; if it were not so, I would have told you. I am going there to prepare a place for you. And if I go and prepare a place for you, I will come back and take you to be with me that you also may be where I am. You know the way to the place where I am going. (John 14:1–4)

Without faith there is no real peace, says Jesus. The gospel is not a package of ethical truths to be applied in the abstract. The values of the kingdom of God derive from the Son of God, by whom and in terms of whom these promises were made.

But 'when he had finished praying, Jesus left with his disciples and crossed the Kidron Valley' (18:1). They were on the last stretch of the way of the cross. Gethsemane was a short walk away.

The church is not to expect to be untroubled

In the love of Jesus the church will be eternally secure, but there will be a cost, as Paul was to remind his Roman readers years later:

> Who shall separate us from the love of Christ? Shall trouble or hardship or persecution or famine or nakedness or danger or sword? As it is written:
>
> 'For your sake we face death all day long;
> We are considered as sheep to be slaughtered.'
>
> No, in all these things we are more than conquerors through him who loved us. For I am convinced that neither death nor life, neither angels nor demons, neither the present nor the future, nor any powers, neither height nor depth, nor anything else in all creation, will be able to separate us from the love of God that is in Christ Jesus our Lord. (Romans 8:35–39)

Paul takes it for granted that a Christian will experience trials and tribulations. It is because the church is identified with Jesus. Its values are different values from those of the world in which it lives. It could not be otherwise, for to the world, Jesus is somebody to be hated (15:18–25). Even if the church decided to take no interest in the affairs of the world, it would find the world taking a decided interest in the church.

The church is to seek kingdom values

Those who follow Jesus will hate what he hated and will make his priorities their own. For example, in today's world, where the values of popular television are frequently at odds with biblical values, Christians have a mandate from Jesus to seek for different values.

Take, for example, the values of popular television, as seen in the themes and storylines that are considered entertaining. On a typical Sunday (10 April 1994), *The Radio Times* announced:

> *7.50 Ain't Misbehavin'*
> Another episode in the comedy series about marital infidelity . . . Who is that following Dave? Why does everybody keep running into Chuck Purvis, private detective?

On the same day, the ITV Teletext service provided summaries of recent soap opera episodes, of which the following are typical:

> *Eastenders:* Phil discovered Willmott-Brown was in prison for rape. Michelle gave Robbie a public dressing-down. A deeply-troubled Frank went for a walk.
> *Brookside:* Max was concerned about Barry's commitment to the restaurant. Carol thought Mick and Marianne had split up. Jimmy used Barry's money for the heroin.
> *Home and Away:* Tug went for an interview only to find the job had gone. Shane and Kevin stole painting canvas from the Surf Club. Luke and Roxy could not get on.

A great deal is said today about sex and violence on television, and obviously the plot summaries are written to titillate people into watching. And it is also true that soap opera is not wholly absorbed in sex and violence, and provides some of the recreational entertainment that books did in earlier times. Some of the values of soap opera – its sporadic compassion, humour and fine acting, for example – are good values.

But sex and violence are not the only sins that find their way on to television. The sins of greed, pride, acquisitiveness, social snobbery and many more are just as pervasive in the media and perhaps influence the more profoundly because they are less obvious – how many Christians have petitioned the television authorities to reduce the glorification of wasteful lifestyles, family hostility and commercial exploitation on screen?

Of course on Sunday 10 April, as on every Sunday, there was much on television that was good, wholesome and occasionally edifying. The final of the *Young Musician of the Year* competition, for example; a moving documentary about Transylvania; a golden wedding celebration on *Songs of Praise* that teetered just on the right side of schmaltz; and the reliably wholesome *The Cosby Show* – to name but a few. Yet it would be a very naive viewer who did not admit that the overall values of television (because they reflect those of the society that television serves) are not in tune with those of the gospel, though they do from time to time coincide. That does not mean that Christians ought not to own television sets; but it certainly means that television offers a choice of values and the gospel demands that the choice should be carefully made.

What makes gospel values, the values of the kingdom of God, different from secular ones? Not some synthetic concept of 'niceness'; truth is often neither nice nor pretty. Paul reminds us what our priorities should be: 'Whatever is true, whatever is noble, whatever is right, whatever is pure, whatever is lovely, whatever is admirable – if anything is excellent or praiseworthy – think about such things' (Philippians 4:8). Christian values are not to be determined by a majority verdict about what is socially acceptable or inoffensive, but by Christians bringing the light of the Bible to bear on a situation and thinking about that situation with the mind of Christ (Philippians 2:5). It is striking, after reading John 13–17, to notice that Paul's discussion about values follows his earlier words about the peace of God:

> Do not be anxious about anything, but in everything, by prayer and petition, with thanksgiving, present your requests to God. And the peace of God, which transcends all understanding, will guard your hearts and your minds in Christ Jesus. (4:6–7)

Back to Basics?

The implication of the Johannine discourse is that there is no 'bag of values' to which society as a whole should return. We have seen in Chapter 2 how easy it is for people to fight to defend values that happen to reinforce their own security or well-being, and in the process – either deliberately or accidentally – to hallow them and make them absolute. Of course there are certain values that all Christians would agree are essential: compassion, love, service, self-sacrifice, humility, and many more. But they are esteemed not because they are on some check list of desirable values, but because they are practical outworkings of the love of Christ and the character of God. What makes them values worth having is the fact that they are validated by him. Without being grounded in the character of God, values may be good ones but will not achieve a turn-around of public morality. C S Lewis pointed back to 'the old simple principles which we are all so anxious not to see' (p 94). But, as we saw earlier, this did not mean re-adopting a discarded agenda. For Lewis, back to basics meant back to God. We won't have a Christian society, he said, until most of us want it.

The values are the symptom of what is missing, not the thing itself.

In the meantime the church, just as it did in the first century, remains as salt and light in society, being the Body of Christ on earth and demonstrating kingdom values by its life as a community and its life in the community.

Fallen heroes

It is quite probable that the phrase 'Back to Basics', launched with such enthusiasm at the 1993 Conservative Party conference, would have been quietly forgotten after a few months had it not been for the publicity that surrounded the series of revelations about the private lives of a number of prominent Conservative politicians (though the Press diligently sought out revelations about politicians from other parties, too).

The Press coverage varied from studied, responsible articles that made their political points almost by accident, to what amounted in the tabloid Press to hysteria. When it was alleged that the Labour MP Dennis Skinner – a deliciously ambiguous figure in the Press's view, because of his contempt for government and his sometimes aggressively flamboyant moral tirades – had a mistress in a well-heeled suburb, the reporting acquired the flavour of pantomime as photographs appeared on the front pages of a heavily-disguised figure said to Mr Skinner, peering left and right as he approached what was alleged to be the love-nest.

Suddenly everybody seemed to have an opinion about the private morality of politicians. They became the target of everybody's criticism, and the final conclusive proof of the bankruptcy of the government's Back to Basics campaign. At least, so the popular media said.

In Chapter One we suggested that the Bible discourages us from wanting to put our government into the hands of Christians if faith is their only qualification for office. The Law is King, not the King. The task of monarchs, presidents, parliaments and government of any kind is to frame just legislation and carry out fair and compassionate government. The Bible does not teach that the primary qualification for an effective career in politics is to be a born-again Christian, any more than being a Christian automatically qualifies one to be a schoolteacher – though in both cases, the job involves areas of life about which Christianity has a great deal to say, and many Christians have found in politics (and in education too) a way to influence their society towards biblical values. That was the case in the nineteenth century with William Wilberforce and Lord Shaftesbury, and there have been many like them before and since.

The glass pedestal

But that does not mean that politicians are holier than the rest of us, or spiritually more heroic. They are accountable as leaders and if they are Christians they are accountable as Christian leaders, but to put them on a pedestal is to do something that God has not done.

The problem is not confined to politics. When Christians fall, they often fall from high places that they have not always built themselves. In America's 'Electronic Church', there have been much-publicised moral failures of various church leaders, the reverberations of which have not yet completely died away. Yet often when one examines the circumstances one finds a lack of accountability on every level. In some cases there has certainly been lack of financial and moral accountability. But where were the people to whom that person could turn for counselling, for fellowship, for rebuke? Often the church leaders whose disgrace dominated the headlines were revered by their followers and consequently were left severely alone and unchallenged, an isolation facilitated by the sheer size of churches whose 'congregations' were often united only by a television channel.

On a different level it's a danger faced by every congregation, the danger of idolising a leader and then being appalled that he or she turns out to be as frail as the rest of us, and inevitably blaming them for not being what they never claimed to be.

'To err is human . . .'

It would be extremely silly to say that every disgraced politician has been more sinned against than sinning – that it is the fault of those surrounding him that he has chosen to break his marriage vows, father a child by an unmarried woman, etc. But there seems to be an element of this in each of the published stories. And it is right that this should be where we begin, because the Bible is a treatise on forgiveness from Genesis through to Revelation. The gospel's story of the human race is of rebels needing to be pardoned and of a guiltless judge who paid the penalty himself. That theme runs through Scripture and is perhaps most poignant in the parables of Jesus, especially the parable about the Unmerciful Servant (Matthew 18:21–35). In the Bible, 'Freely you have received, freely give' (Matthew 10:8) applies as much to forgiveness as to charity. Christians have the greatest possible reason for compassion: infinite compassion has been shown first to them. Shakespear expressed it well in the words of Isabella in *Measure for Measure*:

> Why, all the souls that were were forfeit once;
> And He that might the vantage best have took
> Found out the remedy. How would you be,
> If He, which is the top of judgement, should
> But judge you as you are? (II.ii)

And this also means that another aspect of the tabloid furore is forbidden ground for Christians; the overtones of envy and vengeance that marked some newspapers' coverage.

The moral issues

Yet in a democracy governments govern by consent, and it is therefore the responsibility of the people to scrutinise those who lead them. Western governments take power because a substantial section of the population have agreed to their manifestos. The democratic process, whether it takes place in a republic or a constitutional monarchy, is one of leaders being accountable to the people, even if the people's voice is effective only at election time. The democratic discussion goes on in and out of Parliament. There are numerous ways of making one's voice heard (some of them are listed in the following pages). And if the people have any power at all, then Christian people have a responsibility to make a Christian contribution to the discussion. So what should we be saying?

The Bible gives us a basis on which to say several things.

First, *we must say that immorality is wrong*. Certainly it is hypocritical to single out fallen politicians as the only sinners, or as worse sinners than oneself, as if God graded sins in some way and put sexual immorality or financial crookedness at the top of the list. And it is very easy to be lulled by those voices in modern society that downplay values of faithfulness, commitment to one's partner, responsibility to one's children, honest dealing with other people's financial investments, and so on. Indeed, there is a disturbing strand of opinion today that almost applauds those who are exposed as adulterers, swindlers and thieves, provided that it is done with style. Against this the Bible is extremely clear (eg Habakkuk 1:13, Romans 1:18–32, etc.).

Second, *we must say that punishment is proper*. Sexual immorality tends to get the biggest headlines, but it is not the only sin that often goes unpunished. Businesses frequently liquidate owing hundreds of thousands of pounds, and make use of loopholes in company law to set up again in exactly the same business, but without having to pay the creditors of their old company. (The earliest public discussion of this was David Frost's famous 'trial by television' of the financier Savundra: to Savundra's protest that he had no *legal* obligation to repay those whose money he had lost, Frost retorted that though may be true, he most certainly had a *moral* obligation to do so.) Often the British legal system works against those without money or influence (a good way to find this out, if you are not well off, is to try suing somebody for libel). Cases such as these are clearly covered by the Bible's consistent urging that the weak and vulnerable in society must be treated with special care. The tragedy of the Maxwell pension fund misappropriation was not the huge amount of money involved in total, but the relatively small monthly pensions which many elderly people will not now receive and for which, in good faith, they had paid.

The Bible makes it clear that this is wrong; it also makes it clear (eg 2 Samuel 12:1–24, Psalm 73, Mark 9:42, etc.) that such wrongdoing must be punished.

Third, *we must say that punishment should aim at restoration*. The church has an opportunity to model values to the world. There have been a number of cases in recent years like the Ealing Vicarage Rape case a few years ago. The statements made since by Jill Saward and her father, Rev Michael Saward, have moved and challenged thousands. A badly battered Michael Saward (at that time understandably keeping his daughter's identity as the victim hidden) spoke from a hospital bed on the television news shortly after the attack. He said that he was very anxious that the attackers should be caught and punished, because what they had done was wrong. But he did not hate them. He wanted them to be helped to change.

The very low emphasis on rehabilitation in current British prison legislation, and the emphasis on custodial sentences rather than on the notion of prison as reformatory, is not a biblical emphasis. It is possible to be naive to the point of sentimentality, and to want prisons to lose any sense of punishment at all; but ought Christians to be satisfied with a prison system that often makes its inmates into more efficient criminals?

The church can offer Peter Baelz's 'symbolic pattern of government' here too, for James's instructions on treating offenders within the church are very relevant:

My brothers, if one of you should wander from the truth

and someone should bring him back, remember this: Whoever turns a sinner from the error of his way will save him from death and cover over a multitude of sins. (James 5:19–20)

Fourth, *we must say that political ability is no vindication.* A disturbing trend in recent years has been for disgraced politicians to be restored to their government posts, after a token resignation, with indecent haste. The reason given by the Prime Minister of the day has invariably been that the political abilities of the person in question are so considerable that the cabinet or the Parliamentary Party ought not to be denied the benefit of them for a minute longer than necessary.

A much-quoted example during the 'Back to Basics' controversy was that of John Profumo, who left his cabinet post after the notorious 'Profumo Affair' that is often said to have brought down the Macmillan government. He then worked in the East End of London on social welfare projects, and succeeded in rehabilitating himself in public opinion. The Press approval of his withdrawal from public life was somewhat suspicious; there may have been a hint of a desire for revenge, a feeling that service in the East End was more an (admittedly self-imposed) exile than an honourable rehabilitation. One wonders whether the Press and public would have been prepared to have seen Profumo rehabilitated, if that meant that he once again played a part in the government of the country. Nevertheless the comparison between Profumo, who departed like a gentleman, and disgraced politicians in 1993/4 who appeared to be clinging to office at all costs, was pointed out with some ribaldry.

Yet it is true that Profumo's ministerial gifts do not seem to have been considered a reason for not accepting his resignation. He had done something which was morally wrong, and he had to pay the prescribed punishment. It was a much simpler system in those days, and it's hard not to see it as a more biblical one – provided that one sees punishment as containing at least an element of rehabilitation.

At such points the church's 'symbolic pattern of government' may well have something to offer secular observers. What happens in churches when a leader is disgraced for moral failure? In most biblically-founded churches discipline would mean the immediate suspension of any priest, elder or church officer who was convicted by church or state of immoral behaviour. It would be considered quite wrong for such a person to go on instructing others in how to live their lives. But the suspension would be only the beginning of a programme of rehabilitation. The offender would be disciplined, but also counselled and helped. The aim would be, as the passage from James quoted above shows us, to keep the person within the fellowship. If the offender were to leave the fellowship it would be in a sense a failure of the church. All church discipline taught in the New Testament is aimed at the restoration of the offender, and a church that had grappled with the Scriptures on this subject should be willing to see a disgraced minister or priest once again welcomed to the ministry, if the church as a whole and the leadership felt that this was the will of God.

It's a far cry from the token resignation or the sideways move that modern politics often uses to deal with moral embarrassments. But in many recorded cases, it works extremely well.

7

PUTTING IT INTO ACTION

Because the gospel is highly practical about these matters we end this book with a highly practical chapter. As we have seen, the church is not intended to provide technical expertise, but to offer principles that can be applied to situations. We have also mentioned the concept of the church modelling a symbolic pattern to the world, providing by its own structures and values 'resources of hope' to those who observe. But how do we, for ourselves as individuals, start to apply the principles to cases? What can we do for example, as individuals and as churches, to further the debate about public morality? If it is true that leaders are morally accountable, how can we foster an atmosphere of moral scrutiny? And if we feel that society is rapidly losing moral values – and that the values to which our society holds have lost their spiritual grounding – how may such values be regained or re-grounded?

The poet Coleridge (of whom it has been said that he could have competently held university professorships in at least five subjects[94]) suggested in *Aids to Reflection. . . . on the Several Grounds of Prudence, Morality and Religion* that

94. I'm grateful to Peter Cousins not only for this comment, but for directing my attention to Coleridge's prose writings when I was a schoolboy.

one way was to look first at our own understanding of our faith.

> There is one sure way of giving freshness and importance to the most common-place maxims – that of reflecting on them in direct reference to our own state and conduct, to our own past and future being.[95]

If, as we have seen, the church is a group of like-minded individuals rather than a corporation with a 'party line' (except insofar as it speaks on matters that might be regarded as central to the Christian gospel), Coleridge's point is surely a good one. The church is not a building, or a vicar, or even a bishop or archbishop. The church is the individual Christian, meeting with others in a local visible congregation to worship God and witness to him in the power of the risen Jesus Christ and the Holy Spirit. Consequently the most dangerous thing we can do with our faith is to hug it to ourselves, telling nobody but other Christians about it, and making precisely the same difference to the world as if we were not Christians at all. As Coleridge continues,

> To restore a common-place truth to its first uncommon lustre, you need only translate it into action. But to do this, you must first have reflected on its truth.[96]

Christian action is a new area for many and a minefield for most of us. Fortunately, there are a number of helps available, some of which are mentioned in the course of this chapter. In particular a number of books have been written exploring ways in which an individual faith can be translated into social concern. One of these is a book written for students in IVP's 'Frameworks' series. In it, Roy McCloughry

95. S T Coleridge, *Aids to Reflection* (1825), Aphorism II. This book, a collection of marginal and other comments on passages from Christian writers (chiefly Bishop Leighton), had a strong effect on the Christian Socialist movement.
96. Ibid, Aphorism III.

addresses the subject of Christian social action. He provides a check list at the end of his chapter 'Talking tactics':

> Q1. How much time do you have a week for taking on a new commitment? Is the time in the evenings/weekends, or during the day?
> Q2. Are you more interested in social and political work or in personal work?
> Q3. Are you more focused on local or national issues?
> Q4. List 3 local issues which you are interested in.
> Q5. Is there any particular group of people who you are interested in working with (e.g., the elderly, the disabled, etc.)?
> Q6. What kind of skills do you have to offer? (Remember that even something like a driving licence can be important.)
> Q7. What 3 national issues do you feel most strongly about? Do you already belong to, or have links with, groups which are taking up these issues?
> Q8. Would you be prepared to put some money aside, either to help a cause or to provide you with information? If so how much?
> Q9. What do other people think about your plans? How will they fit in with family life?
> Q10. If you are a Christian, how do you think your choices should reflect your Christian faith?
> Q11. To what extent are you prepared for your lifestyle to change if you are taking on an interest such as 'Green Issues'?[97]

I would like to use this check list (which is one of several in McCloughry's extremely helpful book) as a starting point.

97. Roy McCloughry, *Taking Action: The Practical Guide to Making an Impact in Society* (IVP Frameworks, 1990), p 23.

Costliness

A significant number of McCloughry's questions involve some kind of sacrifice: Q1, of time; Q5, of commitment; Q6, sharing one's skills; Q8, financial commitment; Q9, possible family problems; Q11, possible change in lifestyle. To these might have been added the distinct possibilities of losing the sympathy of friends, of appearing to be a busy-body or trouble-maker, and of putting in long hours and a massive emotional commitment with very little recognition or appreciation. Taking action, making a difference, is not a soft option and it is not an inexpensive hobby.

Of course it was exactly the same for the early church, once that initial honeymoon period of popularity had passed. Once people realised that not only were these people intent on shattering long-standing social taboos, on confronting authorities with the fact of social injustice, and even on accusing national rulers to their face of immorality and immoral leadership; and once it was realised that this agenda was being followed because the followers of the new Way were worshippers of one who was said to be a crucified criminal who had claimed to be a national deliverer; then the hostility began in earnest, and it began to be costly to be a Christian. Read Hebrews 11. As Jesus had warned his disciples, so it turned out:

> You must be on your guard. You will be handed over to the local councils and flogged in the synagogues. On account of me you will stand before governors and kings as witnesses to them. And the gospel must first be preached to all nations. Whenever you are arrested and brought to trial, do not worry beforehand about what to say. Just say whatever is given you at the time, for it is not you speaking, but the Holy Spirit. Brother will betray brother to death, and a father his child. Children will rebel against their parents and have them put to death.

> All men will hate you because of me, but he who stands firm to the end will be saved. (Mark 13:9–13)

Priorities

Christian action is costly, but that does not mean that every Christian should take up every worthy cause. McCloughry's list is intended to help his readers establish priorities, especially questions Q2, Q4, Q7 and Q9. There are wider factors to be considered too as one establishes one's priorities.

It is certainly not the case that the only effective action to change society is that which takes place in the Houses of Parliament or in other places where government is enacted. It is possible that somebody who possesses the gifts and skills to operate effectively in such an environment may actually be required by God to operate in a much less public arena. Changing the world is a very practical matter, and it is inextricably part of the gospel, as Sherwood Eliot Wirt pointed out a quarter of a century ago in his influential *The Social Conscience of the Evangelical*:

> The new translations also reveal in a fresh way that the Apostle James had a highly sensitized social conscience. 'Now what use is it, my brothers, for a man to say he "has faith" if his actions do not correspond with it? Could that sort of faith save anyone's soul? If a fellow man or woman has no clothes to wear and nothing to eat, and one of you say, "Good luck to you," . . . what on earth is the good of that?' James has many provocative things to say about Christians putting into practice the message they have received from Jesus. He makes explicit what is implicit all through the New Testament: that the Christian social conscience should be as wide as the love of God in Christ. It belongs on the same plane as his ecumenical sense of fellowship in the Gospel, for that fellowship is founded on an evangelistic outreach to all men. Jesus

> Christ preached to the multitudes, he had compassion on the multitudes, he died for the multitudes. As he was in the world, so also are we.[98]

It may be objected that the discussion is straying away from public and private morality into the different field of social action. But the two are closely linked. Caring for the needy, feeding the starving, providing for the poor, visiting the lonely and similar activities are practical expressions of compassion and charity, without which no society can be termed 'Christian'. It might be tempting to use this fact to criticise the Conservative government which is in power as I write; for several years now its policy has been effectively to privatise aspects of charity and welfare, so that its critics argue that individuals are having to shoulder the burden that should be borne by the state. But it is worth remembering C S Lewis's point (p 95), that the Christian duty of charity is not cancelled by state provision for the needy.

Every Christian, therefore, has prayerfully to work out priorities, but charity and compassion must be part of the life of every Christian. Some who would wish to campaign in the streets will find that their priority is the care of an elderly relative; some who would have liked to teach in a primary school will find themselves encouraged to stand for local or national political office, and their life will take a quite different direction to what they had expected. Relatively few people end up as they thought they would. But nobody finds themselves in a situation, either of God's or their own choosing, where it is not possible to practise charity and compassion.

98. Sherwood Eliot Wirt, *The Social Conscience of the Evangelical* (Scripture Union, 1968), p 7. The translation of James 2–14 is by J B Phillips.

Organisations

McCloughry's check list (Q7, Q8) mentions organisations. Most of us find it helpful to associate with others who share our concerns. Organisations provide support for individuals; resources that are too expensive for a single campaigner (such as publishing facilities, accountancy, mailing etc.); a ready-made group of fellow-campaigners; and above all a voice. Organisations as different as the Evangelical Alliance and the National Viewers and Listeners Association command a hearing even from those who disagree with their agenda. Broadcasters, commercial interests, local governments and a wide range of other authorities and powers will often take note if an organisation representing several hundred thousand individuals makes representations.

It would of course be quite wrong to ignore secular organisations working in the areas in which one is interested. Common sense alone would dictate otherwise, for many have Christian origins, many have Christians in their leadership, and, too, no sensible Christian organisation would duplicate work being done competently and effectively by a secular equivalent (though where there is more work to be done than organisations existing to do it, such as in international famine relief, it is no surprise to see a number of Christian organisations active).

Organisations founded and maintained by Christians are the only ones operating within a Christian worldview and drawing their rationale from the Bible. But a Christian will often find that though a secular organisation does not share his or her priorities, it may share many of the same concerns. Here are two examples:

A lobbying organisation formed to campaign for justice in inner city housing might be funded and be heavily influenced by a religious group that was explicitly anti-Christian. So a Christian may well come to a point where, however strong the shared commitment to the housing needs of impoverished and disadvantaged communities, working together became impossible. Again, an organisation doing valuable work in the care of AIDS patients and campaigning for adequate medical and care provisions for them, might at the same time be militantly advocating sexual lifestyles with which a Christian might have major disagreements.

Francis Schaeffer used the useful term 'co-belligerency', by which he meant that it is possible to work side by side with organisations with which one has substantial agreement, provided that disagreements on other matters are not so severe as to make the association a betrayal of one's fundamental convictions.

> Christians must realise that there is a difference between being a co-belligerent and an ally. At times you will seem to be saying exactly the same thing as the New Left elite or the Establishment elite. If there is social injustice, say there is social injustice. If we need order, say we need order. In these cases, and at these specific points, we would be co-belligerents. But do not ally yourself with either of these camps: you are an ally of neither. The Church of the Lord Jesus Christ is different from either.[99]

Group campaigning

A wide range of issues can be effectively addressed by Christians working as a group: for example, famine relief, local housing schemes, disability projects, amenity provision, etc. An example in my own experience is the small organisation I and my wife have formed with another couple in our church, to raise money for, and otherwise support, Christians in Transylvania.

In fact our little group demonstrates some of the points that need to be thought through.

1. *Don't re-invent the wheel.* The excitement of having a

99. Francis A Schaeffer, *The Church at the End of the Twentieth Century* (Norfolk Press, 1970), p 46.

project of one's own can make it easy to forget that other, larger organisations can do the job more effectively. Might your group work better as a local catchment for a bigger organisation, so that the costs are spread more widely? We no longer take goods to Romania ourselves, since we discovered that organisations taking huge lorries across were willing to deliver our goods for a very reasonable charge that was far more cost-effective than taking a small van.

2. *Don't ignore help.* Many national organisations provide invaluable resources for local groups; for example CARE has action packs on pornography and other subjects, Christian Impact will help you set up local conferences, Evangelical Alliance offers various services, and all these will cost you a lot less than originating your own. We have benefited greatly from working with an international Christian organisation based in Eastern Europe.

3. *Join forces when you can.* The Christian church is afflicted as much as any organisation with a tendency to go it alone. Fellowship, support, prayer and local know-how are all benefits of being part of a network. Contacts with Christians in other churches can lead to whole new initiatives developing. We have benefited from the enthusiasm of other local churches, some of whom have contributed substantially to our projects.

4. *Select your priorities, identify your niche.* We decided to concentrate on the most visited part of Transylvania but look for areas of need there that had been overlooked by aid convoys heading East. The decision meant deciding not to pursue a number of other objectives that we were attracted to and of which we could well see the importance. But a small group can only do so much.

5. *Periodically assess your group's effectiveness.* A small group should be willing to disband as soon as it has done what it set out to do, or if it reaches a point where it is no longer able to fulfil its aims.

Campaigning as an individual

There is a very wide choice of ways to make a difference as an individual. You can become a speaker on local issues or on topics about which people need to be informed and alerted. You can write letters and encourage others to do so. You can look for ways to appear on television and radio – which is easier than it looks. Television chat-shows (especially day-time ones), radio phone-ins, and opportunities such as Channel 4's *Right to Reply* all invite contributions from the public. Local radio, too, thrives on local opinions.

Letters to local newspapers can mobilise public opinion, and writing to MPs and other people in positions of authority can be effective too. Personal lobbying is a recognised way of making the government know your position, though this is most effective if a number of people lobby together. Your town hall and local councillors are also points of access to the political process.

For some, standing for election to local or national politics will be the most effective way of getting things done. Others will join Trade Unions, party organisations, pressure groups and other political groups – often these make more effective platforms than the parliamentary back benches.

The above are just a few possibilities out of many. Though they are not exhaustive, they show that there is a continuous dialogue going on between the people and the politicians. If we feel that our society needs to change direction, or that the actions of a particular politician are wrong, or that as a society we no longer hold certain values to be important, we are not doomed to be unheard. Of course the necessary qualities of conciseness, lack of arrogance, use of proper channels, grasp of facts, avoidance of rhetoric and all the rest are important, but the access is there if one looks for it.

But we finish with the image to which we have referred several times, of the church modelling resources of hope and symbolic patterns of government to the world. Though Christian action is important, what speaks loudest and changes the world most effectively is changed lives. The early church was the greatest force for change in the ancient world. It outlived the Roman empire that persecuted it. It spread faster than armies and had more courage.

In societies crumbling from greed and bitterness, it restored communities of love and compassion. It stood up to corrupt rulers and took up the cause of runaway slaves. It was fearless in preaching. In an age of secret religions its gospel was a public gospel, and when learning and civilisation passed into a dark age it was one of the few sources of faith and culture.

For this, its saints through the ages were harassed and persecuted and even sawn in two. Yet it was a community marked by one extraordinary quality; that of love. In loving God they loved each other. It was a love that bred compassion and still does. In Eastern Europe today the church is frequently recognised by secular governments as one of the few effective agents of social care, and when the disgraced East German leader Honecker fled from those he had exploited, he was given food and shelter and medical help by a Christian family.

Of course values such as kindness, integrity, loyalty, personal morality and good relationships are not restricted to the Christian community alone.

But the biblical view of human beings as the image-bearers of God suggests that for people of all faiths and of none, 'basic values' must be a spiritual, not a pragmatic, matter.

The values are wonderful, but not one of those early believers would have thought of them as 'basics'. They were simply the values of the Kingdom: what you did if you loved the Lord. From him, in the end, all good moral values came; going 'back to basics' meant going back to him.

It still does.